AAK— 9114

Ackoff's Fables

Ackoff's Fables

IRREVERENT REFLECTIONS ON BUSINESS AND BUREAUCRACY

RUSSELL L. ACKOFF

JOHN WILEY & SONS, INC.

New York • Chichester • Brisbane • Toronto • Singapore

Copyright © 1991 by Russell L. Ackoff
Published by John Wiley & Sons, Inc.

Library of Congress Cataloging-in-Publication Data

Ackoff, Russell Lincoln
    [Fables]
    Ackoff's fables : irreverent reflections on business and
bureaucracy / Russell L. Ackoff.
        p.   cm.
    ISBN 0-471-53194-4
    1. Bureaucracy—Anecdotes. 2. Business—Anecdotes.
3. Bureaucracy–Humor. 4. Business—Humor. I. Title.
HD38.4.A27   1991
650'.0207—dc20   90-48565

Printed in the United States of America.

91 92 10 9 8 7 6 5 4 3 2 1

❧ ❧ ❧

My wife Alexandra,
who is frequently referred to in the fables,
died in 1987.
She had shared most of my past.

This book is dedicated to Helen,
whom I subsequently married
and with whom I hope to share all of my future.

Preface

Development is now generally taken to be what Winnie the Pooh called a Good Thing. Nevertheless, few know what development means or how it differs from growth. Even fewer are aware of the pervasive obstructions to its attainment. It is my contention that most systems created to promote development actually prevent or retard it. Therefore, if we want to maximize our personal development or that of the groups to which we belong, we must learn how to beat these obstructive systems.

There is no subject of which I am aware that is simultaneously as serious and as much fun as beating the system. *The system* referred to in this expression is generally a bureaucracy. Nothing is as obstructive to the satisfaction of human needs and desires, let alone human progress, as bureaucracies. Therefore, beating them has become essential for those who want to develop as rapidly as possible. Nevertheless, there is no educational system—most of which are perfect exemplifications of obstructive bureaucracies—that offers courses on this subject. This is a deficiency for which I try to compensate in this book.

Having done some teaching about development and obstructions to it, I have learned that students remember relevant stories about these subjects much better than they remember the principles I have used to illustrate them. This is true for most subjects. Therefore, the older I've become the more I've used stories to help me make points in lectures, discussions, and writing. When I meet former students, many of whom are now miraculously older than I, I find they remember my stories even when they have forgotten what point they were used to illustrate. Some have reworked the stories creatively and used them to illustrate their own points. Although they may not have learned from the stories what I had intended, they learned something by using them. This is more than I can say about the principles I've promoted. Therefore, I decided that here I would turn the usual way of presenting ideas upside down:

Stories are commonly used to support or embellish the presentation of subject matter. In this book I use subject matter to embellish stories. The stories were written first; then the supporting text was prepared.

All but a few of the stories are essentially true. They tell of my personal experiences. I have told them so many times, however, that they are bound to have evolved in the retelling; in addition, I've dramatized and condensed them a bit. This is why I call them "fables." A fable is *a very short story with a very sharp point*, or, according to my friend and mentor Tom Cowan, *a story that may not be true, but ought to be.*

I have embellished the stories to sharpen their points. All fables have a point, a lesson to convey. This is not true of many stories and most discussion. Therefore, I have used discussion only to illuminate the points of the fables.

The point of the points I try to make in this book is not so much to extract uncritical agreement from readers but to stimulate their critical thinking. In addition, I wanted to provide some fun. Stories, unlike discussion, are often sources of pleasure. A story that isn't, isn't worth telling, however sharp its point.

RUSSELL L. ACKOFF

Philadelphia, Pennsylvania
March 1991

Contents

Teachers kill creativity by inducing students to give them the answers that students think teacher expect. Answers that are expected cannot be creative . . . The right information can't be extracted from the wrong data . . . Those who can't get on together frequently do so when one of them gets off . . . There are as many realities as there are minds contemplating them . . . One can learn a great deal from one's own mistakes, but practically nothing from those made by others . . . Silence is sometimes more eloquent than words . . . It is very difficult to listen while talking . . . The less we expect from others, the less we are likely to get from them . . . Learning begins with questions we cannot answer; it ends with questions we can . . . All's well that ends well, not begins well

When a distinction that does not exist makes a difference, it's more a matter of a distorted mind than distorted vision . . . Color is in the eye of the beholder, not in the skin of the beheld . . . Trust is not a gift from others, it is compensation for work done . . . When a distinction, however difficult to make, makes a significant difference, we learn how to make it . . . Few things are as uplifting as a good put-down . . . To the fanatic there is only one belief possible other than his own, and it is necessarily wrong

There is more to solving an old problem than giving it a new twist . . . Some circles are much more vicious than others . . . Asking is not always the best way to obtain an answer to a question . . .

There is no way of resolving conflict between people who agree to disagree and who value that disagreement . . . When nothing can make things worse, doing anything makes them better . . . Opinion's most deadly enemy is fact . . . What others think of us is often more on our minds than theirs . . . It is very dangerous for a sheep to pretend to be a wolf . . . Wrongs are easily righted among friends and rights are easily wronged among enemies . . . Respect should be based on what a person does, and not on any other characteristic

The principal obstruction between man and what he desires most is man himself . . . To be free is to control one's own time; it can be given to, but should never be taken by, another . . . Irrationality is more likely to be found in the mind of the beholder than in the mind of the beheld . . Talking back can sometimes move things forward . . . It is better to walk backward to where one wants to go than to walk forward to where one doesn't . . . One is free to do something only if one controls the consequences of not doing it . . . Cleanliness can have other effects than holiness . . . Giving others a hand often attracts a hand in return . . . The trouble with morality is that it obscures the difference between good and evil

Chapter One

Beating the System

Notes from an Antibureaucrat

❦ ❦ ❦

If you're going to sin, sin against God, not the
bureaucracy. God will forgive you but the
bureaucracy won't.

—Admiral Hyman G. Rickover

The British created a civil service job in 1803 calling
for a man to stand on the Cliffs of Dover. The man
was supposed to ring a bell if he saw Napoleon
coming. The job was abolished in 1945.

—Robert Townsend, *Up the Organization*

The only thing that saves us from bureaucracy is its
inefficiency.

—Eugene McCarthy

❦ ❦ ❦   *Check and Double Check*

Whenever Madge, a London housewife, went shopping, she would stop to cash a check at a large branch of a chain store that was located very near her flat. This saved her walking several blocks to the closest branch of her bank.

One day when Madge stopped at the store to cash her check, she was told that the store had a new policy: no check cashing. She was indignant, but not for long. She went to the dress department of the store and bought a dress priced at approximately the amount of the check she wanted to cash. The store accepted her check in payment for the dress. Madge then took the dress to the return desk and asked for a refund. They gave it to her in cash.

> MORAL: No system is as smart as some of the
> people it serves.

Systems and Variety

What we learn from experience is conditioned by the social systems with which we interact: family, schools, government and its institutions, communities, corporations, and so on. All effects on us of social systems fall into one of two classes: either they enable us to do or have something we could not otherwise do or have, or they prevent us from doing or having something we could otherwise do or have. In other words, the systems with which we interact may either increase or reduce the variety of behavior available to us.

Of course, a system may be enabling in some areas and obstructive in others. For example, a school may enable children to learn a subject they would not otherwise learn, but it may also prevent them from learning something they would learn if left to their own devices. However, most systems can be characterized as predominantly either variety-increasing or variety-decreasing. A prison, for example, is clearly variety-decreasing, while a library is variety-increasing.

Beating Bureaucracy

The most variety-decreasing type of social system is one we call a *bureaucracy*. A bureaucracy is an organization whose principal objective is to keep people busy doing nothing. They are preoccupied with what we call make-work. For example, application for renewal of a driver's license, which takes only a few minutes to process in the state in which I reside, takes hours to process in Mexico. The output is identical in both cases: a card authorizing operation of an automobile. What is being done in the additional time required for the processing in Mexico? Nothing. It could be eliminated with no effect on the output.

The problem created by people who are busy doing nothing is that they frequently obstruct others who have real work to do. They impose unproductive requirements on others. For example, my application for renewal of my driver's license in Pennsylvania requires no signature but my own; in Mexico, I had to collect a large number of signatures of officials before I could submit my application. It sometimes required more than a day to do so.

Bureaucracies obstruct development. They retard improvement of quality of life. For these reasons most efforts directed at beating systems are directed at getting around bureaucracies, trying either to avoid doing what they needlessly require, or to do something that clearly needs doing but that they try to keep from being done.

Bureaucrats want all parts of an organization to conform to one set of rules and regulations. Exceptions to rules, no matter how justified they may be, are anathema to a bureaucracy. Conformity is treated as good in itself, an ultimate good. Because bureaucrats give more attention to obtaining conformity than to what is conformed to, they are sometimes vulnerable.

🐭 🐭 🐭   Equal What?

One of my university's faculty members, who exemplified the bureaucrat, was appointed by the provost to chair a committee to review compensation of graduate students employed to teach or do research. Under his leadership this committee conducted a survey that revealed significant differences in student compensation in different parts of the university. He and his committee learned that students employed in the research group that I directed were the highest paid in the university. The chairman then dedicated himself to "getting" me.

He asked me to appear before his committee. When I did he opened the session with a discourse on the desirability of equity in compensation of students regardless of where or on what they were working. He then asked what I thought about the position he had just formulated, clearly expecting me to disagree with it. However, I said that I agreed completely. This caught him by surprise. It took several minutes of hemming and hawing before he got back on course.

"Then," he said, "you will have no objection to reducing the salary paid to your students to a level equal to that of most other students."

"I certainly would," I said, again surprising him. "I agree to equity, but at the level of compensation that my students receive."

In the discussion that followed it became clear that equity was not the issue; the level of compensation was. I was asked to justify our high level of student compensation. I did so in a way that convinced at least a few on the committee. The chairman broke into the discussion to say that even if our compensation was justified, the National Science Foundation, the principal source of support of students on campus, would not tolerate such compensation as we provided.

He had not done his homework. I revealed that we had two contracts with that foundation and our students' compensation had never been questioned.

Nevertheless, the committee eventually recommended equalization of student compensation at a lower level than we used. The administration, however, decided not to implement it. The fact that a large portion of the overhead applied to our students' compensation went to the university's general fund may have influenced this decision.

> **MORAL: In a bureaucracy, the only thing more important than conformity is income.**

Bureaucracies tend to mechanize procedures, thereby reducing choice. They specify exactly what is to be done in situations that would otherwise require choice. Those who design these procedures assume they know and have taken into account all possible situations. This is not possible for even a smart person, let alone a bureaucrat.

When the assumption that all possible contingencies have been taken into account turns out to be false, those responsible for administering bureaucratic rules or regulations tend to deny the disconfirming evidence. A bureaucratic regulation, like many of the principles taught in school, can withstand any amount of disconfirming evidence.

❦ ❦ ❦   *He or She Shells*

One of my classmates in graduate school was a biological taxonomist who was well known for having developed a widely used system of classifying seashells. I once asked him how he tested this system for its exhaustiveness. He told me that whenever he could, he would visit a beach that he had not previously visited, walk along the shore, and classify each shell he encountered. "Of course," he added, "occasionally I have to step on one."

      **MORAL: To a bureaucrat, an exception to a rule
can be a crushing defeat.**

I had a friend, Glen Camp, who dedicated himself to stepping on the bureaucracies that stepped on the shells that could not be classified. He was the most creative practitioner of this art I have ever known.

❦ ❦ ❦   *A Double Whammy*

Glen Camp, now deceased, was a genius not only at beating systems but at keeping them beat. He was a brilliant and innovative operations researcher who worked on naval problems during World War II. His greatest system-bashing accomplishment occurred when he was assigned to find ways of decreasing the vulnerability of submarines to mines.

Glen went on a submarine mission in the Pacific in order to make observations and collect relevant data. He recorded his data on three-by-five-inch index cards. It was not long before he had a large collection of them. He went to the ship's store and asked for some rubber bands to help him organize his cards. The supply clerk told him there was a war going on and that no rubber bands were available. Glen patiently explained his urgent need for them, but the unsympathetic storekeeper told him to tie the cards together with string. Glen explained that this would be a bother because he had to get at the cards frequently. The storekeeper was unmoved. Glen had to settle for string.

When Glen's submarine returned to the West Coast and its naval base there, he immediately went to the base supply room and again asked for rubber bands. Once again he was told about the war and the shortages it created. Glen was so annoyed by all this that he decided to get even. He found a way to do so: at a five and dime he bought several pairs of women's elastic garters, which did not serve his purpose as well as rubber bands but served it better than string. Glen then turned in a request for reimbursement for the cost of the garters.

The naval officer who processed requests for reimbursement sent for Glen. He said he did not doubt that Glen had purchased several pairs of women's garters, even though he could not imagine what for. However, he said, whatever the reason, the request would never be approved by higher authorities; it was too irregular. He suggested that Glen make out a new request for the same amount, but for something conventional like food or transportation. Glen refused, pointing out that when he signed a request for reimbursement he swore to the truthfulness of the information provided. The frustrated officer reluctantly took Glen's request and passed it on. More than a year passed before Glen received payment for the garters. It had to be approved all the way up to an undersecretary of the navy.

When Glen received the payment, he sold the garters to his secretary for half their original price and prepared a new form returning to the navy the money he had received from this salvage operation.

MORAL: A regulation upheld can hold up the regulated.

The inflexibility and intransigence of bureaucracies can sometimes be turned against them by treating them as unreasonably as they treat you. Clay Hollister, my departmental chairman at Case Institute of Technology, could match the stubbornness of any offending system.

❦ ❦ ❦   *More Than Expected*

Clay did not habitually try to beat systems, but when he did . . . he did so with a vengeance. Sears was the target of one his forays.

He was a dedicated do-it-yourselfer and user of Sears' catalogues. One such catalogue announced a sale. Among the items offered at significantly reduced prices were four-by-eight-foot sheets of quarter-inch Masonite. Although Clay had no immediate need for them, he thought he would eventually and therefore ordered four sheets of Masonite.

One day several weeks later, while Clay was at work, Sears delivered four dozen sheets of Masonite to his home, packed in four heavy wooden crates. Clay notified Sears almost immediately of its error, again by mail. Nevertheless, shortly thereafter and while he still had the entire shipment, he received a bill for four dozen sheets of Masonite. Clay returned the bill to Sears along with a copy of his earlier letter notifying the store of its error. In time he received a letter from Sears offering to credit him for the error if he would return the extra sheets of Masonite by parcel post. Clay wrote back pointing out that the sheets were much too large to send by parcel post and, furthermore, it was Sears' responsibility to pick them up, not his to return them.

Sears ignored Clay's second letter and continued to send bills to him monthly. Interest charges were added and increased with each successive bill because of his failure to pay on time. Eventually Sears threatened to turn the unpaid bill over to a collection agency. Clay retaliated by billing Sears for storage of the 44 sheets of Masonite he had not ordered. Both continued to bill the other over a number of months. Eventually Sears wrote to Clay offering to sell him the extra 44 sheets at a very reduced price. Clay pointed out to Sears that the amount it owed him for storage was now about equal to the price it wanted; he offered to call it even and keep the extra sheets of Masonite. Sears agreed.

MORAL: The best system designer is one who knows how to beat any system that others design.

Bureaucracies, of course, expect complaints from those they victimize, but their responses to complaints tend to be as impersonal as the behavior that instigated the complaint.

❦ ❦ ❦   *A Dirty Word about Taxes*

I once received a computer-prepared letter from a state agency informing me of my failure to pay a tax. I had paid that tax. I indicated this in a return letter in which I enclosed a copy of the check with which I had paid the tax. The state agency ignored my reply and returned another computer-generated letter, more ominous than the first, warning me of the dire consequences of my continuing default. I replied again, this time also enclosing a copy of my previous letter. The third letter I received was also computer generated and oblivious to what had preceded it.

I was no longer amused. The problem was: how to break through the computerized barrier and reach a human being. I did something I had never done before: I wrote a letter in which almost every other word was either profane or obscene. In a postscript to the letter, I explained that I had resorted to such offensive language in the hope that I might elicit a human response. I received a computerized admission of error from the agency, but no apology or sign of a human hand.

**MORAL: The worst thing to do about a
bureaucracy's error may be not to.**

Systems and Service

Service seems to have become a lost art. Systems that are supposed to serve seldom do, and when they do they often do so reluctantly. Employees of such systems become immune to the discomfort and inconvenience they and their systems cause. The only way service can be extracted from many such systems is by force, psychological or physical.

An Overnight Fray

One night I flew into New York City several hours later than my scheduled arrival time because of bad weather, but I had a late reservation (good until midnight) at a prominent hotel. I arrived there at 11:45 P.M. There were about five men waiting in line to register, but only one clerk was on duty. I joined the line, which moved very slowly. I reached the clerk a few minutes after midnight. When I presented him with the confirmation of my reservation he told me that it was no longer valid because it was after midnight. I pointed out that I had arrived before midnight and had been waiting in line since then. Those waiting behind me confirmed my statement. The clerk listened impatiently and then repeated that my reservation was no longer valid, adding that no rooms were available anyhow.

I was infuriated and told the clerk that I would not move from my position in front of him until I had been given a room. He tried to persuade me to move out of the way. When this failed, he threatened to call the night manager and implied there would be dire consequences to me if he did so. I encouraged him to go ahead. He disappeared. (The several men waiting behind me continued their moral support.)

After an absence of about ten minutes the clerk reappeared with the night manager, who had apparently been awakened from a sound sleep. He directed a sequence of increasingly ominous threats at me. I did not budge. When he was convinced that I would not be persuaded to move, he said he was going to call the police. I encouraged him to do so. He and the clerk disappeared.

About ten minutes later they reappeared. The manager said that although he was under no obligation to provide me with a room he was going to do so in order to avoid a scene. He then registered me for a room whose sudden availability he did not explain. When he had finished he obviously expected an expression of gratitude from me. Instead he got an even angrier tirade because, I pointed out, the clerk could have given me that room in the beginning and saved all the subsequent unpleasantness. The manager did not reply. He left angrily and I went to my room.

> ## MORAL: *Few services are good without reservations.*

Why do so many service personnel treat those they are supposed to serve as nuisances, if not enemies? I have found this to be particularly true of airline ground personnel. On many airlines, poor service has been elevated to a fine art. My colleagues and I, all of whom travel by air several times each week, have concocted an imaginary Vice President of Customer Inconvenience to whom we have attributed unlimited ingenuity and perversity. And he trains his airline's personnel almost perfectly.

I recall an evening when I was flying an international airline for whose chief executive officer I was doing some research. I was erroneously bumped from a flight despite having reconfirmed my reservation earlier. The agent would not listen to my protests. I asked him for use of his phone. When he asked why, I said I wanted to call his chief executive officer. He looked at me disbelievingly. After I dialed the number and asked the secretary for the chief executive, the agent disconnected me and promptly put me back on the flight, but not without a great deal of disgruntled mumbling.

Very often when airline personnel are confronted with a customer's problem created by something the airline did, they absolve themselves of any responsibility for the mishap and try to get rid of the inconvenienced customer. They might be forgiven if they did nothing more than show some sympathy.

Of course there are exceptional airline personnel. I encountered one once, an employee of SAS.

❦ ❦ ❦   *Scandinavian Service*

One night I arrived in Stockholm by air several hours late. The airport had been kept open to receive my flight. It began to close once we were off the plane and our baggage had been delivered. I was supposed to be met by a Swedish friend who was to have arranged a hotel for me. He was not there. I waited until the airport had emptied, but he had not appeared. All the airport's change bureaus had closed, so I could not get the coins needed to use the phone. Besides, I did not know his home phone number or his home address, and there were a large number of entries with the same name as his in the telephone directory. In addition, all the taxis had left. The airport appeared to be completely deserted; it was barely illuminated by a few night lights.

I wandered about the airport desperately looking for help. After some time I found an office with a light on. I knocked on the door and was invited in. A young SAS agent was closing shop. I explained my predicament to her. She asked me to sit down and relax. She assured me that she would solve my problem. Then she took a phone book and systematically began to call those with the same name as my friend's. She went through almost a dozen before she reached my friend's wife.

The wife explained that my friend had been called away on urgent business, but several days earlier he had wired me about it and instructed me not to come. I had not received his wire. Then the agent said she would arrange a hotel room for me, and did. She then called a cab, which came to the airport. She explained my situation to the driver and he agreed to wait for payment until I changed some money at the hotel. Off I went, forever grateful to that young lady.

MORAL: No one hath greater love than a satisfied customer.

What a difference between this young lady's attitude and that of the New York hotel's registration clerk. The difference between them was the amount of empathy they had with those they served. The clerk could not see my situation from my point of view, only from his own. The SAS agent clearly identified with me and understood my problem. She treated me as she would like to have been treated in such a situation.

The word *service* derives from the Latin word meaning "slave": service was the work expected of slaves. The rise of Christianity, however, generated an opposing view of service as the highest form of human effort, as exemplified in "service to God." These opposing connotations of service still prevail. In most professions good service ranks as the highest possible accomplishment; it is admired and attracts respect and status. On the other hand, *domestic service* still carries much of its original Latin connotation: slave labor. It attracts little respect or status.

Practice of the arts or crafts contrasts sharply with service. It was and is the work of free people, and it results in tangible products; service produces only effects. In materialistic societies such as ours, the products of arts and crafts have a higher social standing than the effects of service. For these reasons, most forms of social service try to align themselves with such arts and crafts as law, medicine, engineering, and architecture.

What transforms slavelike labor into exalted service are the amount of skill required to provide it; the importance of the need or desire served; the relationship between the server and the served; and prevailing religious, moral, and social opinion. The esteem in which servers and their services are held by the served has a great effect on the quality of service rendered. Servers who view themselves and are viewed by others as necessary evils—or worse still, as unnecessary evils—are unlikely to show much empathy with those they serve. Most airline agents, and the long lines one must stand in to get to them, are viewed as unnecessary evils. (In some cases one's ticket must be shown four times before one can get on a plane.) Hostility to the server by those served generates hostility by the server to those served. This vicious cycle can only be broken by redesigning services so they are arranged for the convenience and comfort of the served and are perceived as such by both the served and the servers.

Removing Systemically Imposed Obstructions

Bureaucracies are almost always aware of their inefficiency, ineffectiveness, and inhumanity. Therefore, they try to keep out of the limelight. This makes them vulnerable to exposure, the threat of which can sometimes work wonders.

❦ ❦ ❦   *Jessie*

The research group and academic department in The Wharton School, of which I was a part until 1986, were located on the fourth floor of a relatively new building, Vance Hall. One of our graduate students employed by the center, Bill Roth, had a wonderful male Labrador retriever, Jessie, who came to work and class with him every day. Every morning Jessie called on each of us in our offices to say hello and collect the treats inevitably provided. When he wanted to go outdoors, he would walk to the bank of elevators at the end of our hall and wait patiently until someone took him down to the ground floor. He reversed the procedure when he wanted to return. He was the most attentive student, and the quietest, in the many seminars he attended.

Jessie was a very important part of our fourth-floor society.

One day, Jessie mistakenly got off the elevator on the third floor and wandered around in a confused state. The professor who directed the center that occupied that floor was very much annoyed by Jessie's presence. He called the university's director of buildings and grounds and told him to remove the dog and prevent his reentering the building. Fortunately, a passing student who knew Jessie retrieved him and returned him to the fourth floor. Nevertheless, a directive was issued by the university prohibiting the admission of pets to our building. A No Pets Allowed sign was posted at each of its entrances.

Jessie, of course, could not read. He continued coming up to the fourth floor, but he was now equipped with a letter I wrote and conspicuously attached to his collar. It read:

> *To whom it may or may not concern:*

> *Jessie, a black, male Labrador retriever who is not my pet but is my friend, and who has been the mascot of the Social Systems*

*Sciences Unit for the last three years, is hereby authorized to enter
and work on the fourth floor of Vance Hall.*

*If anyone has any objections to this authorization, please contact
the undersigned.*

(Signed by me.)

Unfortunately, on one of Jessie's subsequent trips he got on an elevator
occupied by the third-floor director. Shortly thereafter I received a call
from the vice president of the university in charge of facilities telling
me how sorry he was to have to do this, but that he had to prohibit
Jessie's entering our building.

I told him I would comply. However, I invited him to attend a press
conference that I intended to call that afternoon in which I planned to
tell the story of Jessie. I intended to use it as an example of the insidious
dehumanization of the higher educational process. I said I would wel-
come the vice president's giving the university's view of the matter at
that time. His response was profane. Nevertheless, he withdrew his
insistence that Jessie be exiled. I don't know how he handled the third-
floor director, but I heard no more about it.

**MORAL: The power of the press lies more in the
threat of publication than in publication itself.**

Jessie and his owner, Bill Roth, eventually graduated and went
on to their first academic job at Moravian College. Unfortunately, Jessie has since died of old age.

Countermeasures

There is a technique developed by the military either to beat a
system or to design a system that would be difficult to beat. It
consists of forming a "countermeasure team" to represent those
who want to beat the system—the enemy, in the military case.
This team is given all the information available to the good
guys, including tentative designs of the system involved. The
task of the countermeasure team is to develop ways of beating

the system. When it has determined how to do so, the good guys are given this information to use in redesigning their system. After they have done so, the countermeasure team goes at it again. This process continues until the enemy either cannot find an effective countermeasure, or the time required to do so is long enough to justify introduction of the system. The idea behind this procedure is that when a team of intelligent people who have perfect information about a system—something real enemies seldom have—can no longer beat that system quickly enough to make it valueless, that system can be built with little chance of its being beaten.

Note that such a procedure does not reduce the number of choices available to the enemy, but it does reduce their effectiveness. For example, a major national accounting firm once employed the research group of which I was a part to find effective ways of embezzling money from banks so that it could improve its auditing procedures. We found better ways of embezzling than the auditors had dreamed of, but we were able to design new auditing procedures that made our discoveries ineffective. Much to our amazement, the accounting-auditing firm did not adopt these procedures. Its executives said that as long as they used their current procedures, which were approved by the profession, they could not be held legally responsible for thefts they failed to detect. However, if they departed from standardized procedures and failed to detect an embezzlement, they would be legally liable for it. They chose to minimize their risks rather than those of their clients.

In another case, a company that wanted to buy a factory from one of its minor competitors that was going out of business knew that its major competitor was anxious to prevent such a purchase. Acquisition of that factory would increase the competitiveness of the purchaser in a region in which the principal competitor had an advantage. The would-be purchaser employed the research group of which I was a part to act as a countermeasure team while an internal group developed a strategy for obtaining the factory. It took four iterations of the internal group developing an offer and our countermeasure team developing a way of obstructing it before we could no longer find a way of preventing the purchase. Subsequently, when the offer to purchase was made, the principal competitor followed exactly the steps the countermeasure team had taken. The would-be purchaser got the plant.

A smart system can use knowledge of how it can be beat to redesign itself to reduce or eliminate that kind of beating.

☙ ☙ ☙   *Smoke Smuggling*

In the middle 1970s I was asked by a department of the United Nations to visit (prerevolutionary) Iran, to talk with some of its officials about recent developments in the management sciences. I was also asked to help the government with any specific problems it had and to which my experience had some relevance. Several problems were put to me, but the one I remember best involved the purchase and sale of American-made cigarettes.

The minister in charge of consumer affairs told me that the sale of cigarettes in Iran was the second largest source of income to the government, second only to the sale of oil. The government had a monopoly on the legal production, distribution, and sale of cigarettes in Iran. A large and previously increasing portion of the income generated by this business came from the sale of cigarettes imported from the United States, then distributed to and sold through government-licensed retail stores.

In the last few years an illicit trade in American cigarettes had developed, significantly reducing the government's income. Smugglers were buying American cigarettes in Kuwait, where they could be obtained tax-free, and bringing them to Iran in small boats. They were then distributed to unlicensed street vendors who sold them at a price significantly lower than that at which they were sold in government-

licensed outlets. The number of vendors and their share of the market were increasing rapidly.

The minister wanted to know what could be done to eliminate or reduce the smuggled-cigarette business. At my request a small team was set up to deal with the problem. All members of the team except me were familiar with both the legal and illegal cigarette businesses. First, we identified each step in the illicit business and estimated its cost. We were also able to estimate the profit earned by each of the parties involved along the way: the purchaser in Kuwait, the fisherman who brought the cigarettes to Iran, the distributors in Iran, and, finally, the street vendors. Adding the profits obtained by each, we determined the total profit generated by the illegal trade in American cigarettes. Then we did the same for the government's importing, distribution, and sale of American cigarettes. We found that the total profit generated by the government's system was less than that of the illicit system, even though the illicitly sold cigarettes were priced lower.

Therefore, we proposed that the government reorganize its imported cigarette business so as to use the same method of procurement, distribution, and sale the smugglers used. The team pointed out that if the government did so, its profits would probably be even greater than the smugglers', because the government was more likely than the smugglers to avoid having to bribe custom officials and the police.

It is my understanding that these recommendations were followed after I left Iran.

MORAL: It you can't beat a system, join it.

Corruption

Because bureaucracies tend to be inefficient and obstruct development, they invite and encourage corruption. Bribes are required to make them operate less inefficiently and obstructively. Bureaucracies create obstructions for the purpose of eliciting bribes.

❦ ❦ ❦   *On Getting In by Handing Out*

In 1975 my wife and I loaded my VW minivan and, with our dog and cat, headed for Mexico. I had arranged to spend a year as a visiting professor at the National Autonomous University (UNAM) in Mexico City.

I had previously done some work for a Mexican firm located in Monterrey, which was near my planned point of entry into Mexico. That firm offered to send one of its expediters to meet me at the border and help with my entry. I welcomed the offer because it had taken one of my colleagues and his family two days to enter Mexico at that same point.

We were met at the point of entry, Nuevo Loredo, by the expediter, who began the admission process with us. Even with his help it took us eight hours to get cleared for entry. When we were finally permitted to enter, I asked our facilitator how many bribes he had paid. He said, "Sixteen." When I asked him how long it would have taken had he refused to pay any bribes, he said, "Infinity."

MORAL: The shortest distance between some countries is a crooked line.

I had no help in handling most of my subsequent contacts with Mexican varieties of corruption. As a result, I learned that corruption is a way systems have of beating people that people can seldom beat. This was demonstrated to me on my first working day in Mexico City, when I drove from the house I occupied to the university.

❦ ❦ ❦   *On Unlimited Limits*

I drove to work in our VW bus with U.S. license tags on it. A short way from our house I was stopped by two policemen who spoke to me in Spanish, which I could not understand. My lack of understanding did not seem to bother them at all, but it bothered me a great deal because I did not know what was going on. A young man who happened to be passing volunteered to interpret for me. He said the police claimed that I had exceeded the speed limit. I said I had seen no posting of a speed limit. Nevertheless, they told me, I had passed one that established the limit at 35 kilometers per hour. I could not recall having seen such a sign, but there clearly was no use arguing. I told the police to go ahead and make out a ticket for me. They were reluctant to do so; they said they could save me a lot of trouble by collecting the fine right there. I said I preferred to have a ticket. After some dispute about this, one of the policemen asked for my wallet. When I handed it to him he emptied it of all but a few pesos. He then returned it to me and told me to get going.

I went back over the route I had taken before being stopped by the police and looked for the posting of the speed limit to which they had referred. I could not find it.

When I returned home that evening, I warned my wife about the place at which I had been stopped. The next day, when she was driving the same car through the same area, she was stopped by the same policemen. Unlike me, she could manage a bit in Spanish. The police told her she had been exceeding the speed limit. She said she hadn't because I had warned her about the 35 kilometer limit. They told her that the limit had been lowered the previous night to 25 kilometers, and proceeded to extract their bribe from her.

MORAL: The more corrupt a culture, the greater are the out-of-pocket expenses required to live in it.

Corruption occurred at all levels in and out of the Mexican government. However, Mexicans appeared to me to be less bothered by it than North Americans. Their attitude toward it was very different from that of gringos. A Mexican friend explained it to me as follows: In the United States we tip those who serve us after being served, and the amount of our tip reflects our evaluation of the service received. In Mexico the steps are the same but their order is changed: One tips in advance, and the size of the tip determines the quality of service received. In Mexico, the "tip-in-advance" is called a *mordida*, a bite.

I realize, of course, that there is a great deal of corruption in the United States. How can any American be unaware of this? However, in the United States corruption once exposed is seldom tolerated or left unpunished. In Mexico it is taken for granted, treated as a fact of life.

I spent a good deal of time reflecting on the nature and causes of corruption while in Mexico. Later, after I had returned to the States, an agency of the Mexican government sponsored the preparation of a monograph on the subject by my university colleagues and me. We concluded that corruption occurs when one party, A (for example, a policeman), who has an obligation to a second party, B (for example, the government), to provide service to a third party, C (for example, a member of the public), serves C in such a way as to benefit A more than he or she is supposed to. In addition, anyone who induces another to behave corruptly is corrupt. Therefore, corruption is the exploitation for one's personal benefit of a position in which one is expected to serve others.

The immorality of corruption is not nearly as bothersome to me as is its obstructiveness to development. It is a special kind of obstruction, a meta-obstruction, because it is a response to the existence of other obstructions to development. If development were not obstructed, as it is even in the most developed countries, there would be no corruption, because there would be no need for it. To remove the obstructions to a society's development not only promotes development but it also reduces corruption.

The three principal obstructions to societal development, and hence the three principal producers of corruption, are *scarcity of resources, maldistribution of resources,* and *insecurity.* By a resource I mean anything, physical or mental, that can be used to obtain something else that one needs or desires. Therefore, information, knowledge, and understanding are resources as much as is money.

Scarcity of resources is an obvious obstruction to development. Those who have little or none of a resource they need are more easily corrupted than those who have what they need. For example, peasants who wanted the money, seeds, fertilizers, and equipment necessary to grow crops and who approached a branch of Mexico's rural development bank were told they could have what they wanted if they applied for more than they needed. When they received more than they needed they had to give the difference back to the loan officer. He, in turn, released them from an obligation to repay their loan to the bank. Compliance was the most effective way for peasants to get the resources they needed. This practice obviously reduced the amount of resources available for distribution to peasants and therefore retarded rural development. (It is my understanding that this practice has been eliminated since my extended stay in Mexico.)

Even where there is enough of a resource to go around, many may not have enough of it because it is distributed inequitably. Those who do not have enough want more and may be disposed to corruption to obtain it. Those who have more than they want are inclined to protect themselves against a possible future shortage by hoarding it, and through corruption to increase their security. It is commonplace, particularly in countries in which entertainment is a scarcity, for people to pay bribes to obtain tickets from those who hoard them. Those who hoard them often solicit bribes from those who want them. Tickets to special events, artistic or athletic, are made available at a cost considerably greater than their face value.

Where there is a scarcity of resources and maldistribution of what is available, those who have some or even enough resources often feel insecure, threatened. They want to protect what they have against possible loss or appropriation. This is often most easily accomplished through corruption. For example, employees who feel insecure about their jobs where employment is hard to get may give a portion of their salaries to their bosses in order to increase their job security.

Laws, Rules, and Regulations

In some cases a system can be beaten by rigorously following its rules and regulations. English workers know this when they "work to rule." Employee adherence to rules is often more harmful to an employing organization than is a strike. Moreover, those who work to rule do not have to give up their income to make their points. Similarly, most managers know that the easiest way to bring an organization to its knees is to interpret its budget literally. Most organizations survive only because their managers have learned how to cheat with respect to their budgets.

There is something diabolically satisfying in beating a system by adhering to its rules. Here are a few such cases.

❦ ❦ ❦   *On Pants That Don't Suit*

In the early 1950s my wife and I lived in Washington, D.C., where I spent six months as a consultant to the U.S. Bureau of the Census. One evening, together with a census colleague and his wife, we went out to dinner. We had selected a popular seafood restaurant located on the riverfront. Both wives were attractively dressed in pantsuits, which were then just coming into vogue.

When we approached the restaurant's hostess to be seated, she informed us that women wearing pantsuits were not allowed in the restaurant;

they were not considered to be properly dressed. When we asked why, she told us, in effect, that hers was not to reason why but to do or die. She was simply following orders.

Our wives were not upset by their exclusion. They excused themselves and mysteriously disappeared. They went to the ladies' room, took off their pants, and reappeared wearing only the tunics that formed the upper parts of their suits. The tunics were about the length of mini-skirts. The hostess was satisfied and seated us.

MORAL: Taking off one's pants may skirt the issue.

Beating a system by taking it literally is wonderfully illustrated by the story of the Yale freshman who, when he appeared at the freshman dining hall on his first day there, saw a sign at its entrance reading Jacket and Tie Required. On the next day he appeared wearing a jacket and tie—and nothing else.

Systems would much rather be told lies that preserve their conventions than truths that shake them up.

❦ ❦ ❦   *On Disjoint Authorship*

When I was getting ready to start work on my doctoral dissertation, I learned of an obscure and very infrequently used university rule that permitted dissertations to be written jointly by the degree candidate and his or her supervisor. I had not known this and no one I knew at the university was aware of it. Nevertheless, I approached my supervisor, Professor C. West Churchman, with the suggestion that he coauthor my thesis. Much to my surprise and delight, he agreed. (This began a collaboration that lasted almost 20 years.)

Over the next several years, including the four I spent in the army during World War II, West and I produced a document of about 600 single-spaced typed pages. I submitted it to the chairman of the graduate faculty in philosophy. He returned it to me almost immediately, saying that jointly authored theses were not permitted. I was prepared for such a response. I showed the chairman a copy of the relevant university regulation. It shocked him. He didn't believe it, so he checked and found the rule to be valid. He treated me as though I had committed a sin in discovering its validity.

The chairman informed me that the examining committee would have to know which portions of the thesis I had written alone, so I could be examined on them. I explained that Churchman and I had written every part of that thesis collaboratively. Nevertheless, he said, the committee would be unwilling to examine me unless I could provide an example of my independent contribution to the work.

West and I discussed this requirement and decided to designate a particular section. Like all other sections, it had been jointly written, but I did not so inform the committee, which was satisfied. It examined me on that section and reluctantly accepted the thesis as a whole.

> **MORAL: The best response to an arbitrary requirement is one that is itself as arbitrary as the requirement.**

Law and lawyers can be very effective allies of bureaucracies that want to keep anything from happening, but they can be double-edged swords.

❦ ❦ ❦   *On Laws and Lawyers*

After a fruitful day of collaborative problem-solving, a corporation's top executives and academic consultants were relaxing over a few after-dinner drinks. The chief executive officer of the corporation turned to one of the consultants, Tom Cowan, a retired professor of jurisprudence, and asked, "Tom, how come whenever I ask our lawyers whether I can try something new, they always say, 'No'?"

Tom replied, "You deserve that kind of reply because you're asking the wrong kind of question."

"I don't understand," the executive said.

"Let me explain," Tom said. "Why do you consult lawyers?"

The executive looked puzzled, shrugged his shoulders, and replied, "For the obvious reasons: to advise me on legal matters and to represent us in suits that either we initiate against others or they initiate against us."

Tom snapped back, "Come on, you're not testifying in court now. I'm not asking how you use lawyers, but what *you use them for. What is the principal reason for surrounding yourself with lawyers?"*

The executive thought for a moment and then replied, "I suppose you mean: to avoid legal problems, to keep me out of jail."

"Right! Now, consider: When you consult a lawyer, you're not in jail. Then you ask him if you can do something other than what you have been doing. The one thing he knows for sure is that you have not gotten into trouble for not doing what you propose doing. Therefore, to make sure you stay out of trouble, he says, 'No.' He is paid not to take risks, but to minimize them. It's your job to take them."

"Okay," the executive said. "I get your point. Then what *should I ask the lawyer?"*

"Don't ask him anything; tell him: 'I'm going to do so-and-so. Now you tell me how to do it without getting into trouble.' And he probably will. You see, most decision-makers do not use lawyers to enable them to do what they want to do, but to keep them from doing what they don't want to do."

> **MORAL: Lawyers keep those who employ them from doing many illegal or stupid things, but not from using lawyers.**

Laws, rules, and regulations are often written by lawyers. The one thing no lawyer will do, and few other than lawyers can do, is write a law, rule, or regulation that deprives other lawyers of possible work. A better lawyer than the one who wrote a law, rule, or regulation can usually find a way around it, and there is always a better lawyer around.

❦ ❦ ❦   *Obscured Clearance*

Many years ago the university-based research group that I directed negotiated a large contract with the U.S. Arms Control and Disarmament Agency (ACDA). About a week after the contract had been signed, sealed, and delivered, I received a carton full of clearance-application forms that every member of my group was supposed to fill out and submit.

The requirement for clearances had never been discussed during contract negotiations; it came as a complete surprise to me. I called the agency's contracting officer and told him that we would not fill out the applications because we saw no reason for doing so. I explained that the work we had agreed to do was not classified, hence would not require access to classified information. Moreover, only a few members of my group would be involved in the research; most would not. A number of the group's members were not citizens of the United States, and I was not about to put them through the extended indignity of clearance procedures, particularly ones that served no useful purpose.

The contracting officer told me that the law that created ACDA required that it use the same security measures as were required of the Atomic Energy Commission, and these required clearance of all members of my group.

I told the contracting officer that we were not willing to comply with that requirement, whatever its source. He then said that he had no alternative but to cancel the contract. I told him that cancellation was not the only alternative: the agency could engage a good lawyer who would figure out how to get around the law. He dismissed my suggestion as facetious. The contract was cancelled.

A few weeks later I received a call from the agency telling me the contract was being reinstated and that clearance would not be required of any member of my group. No explanation was provided.

❦ ❦ ❦

I had a similar experience when I agreed to address a group of army generals who were going to meet at Duke University. Subsequently, I received a clearance-application form and a request from the army to fill it out. I called the officer who had invited me to the meeting and told him I would not comply because my talk would contain no classified material and I did not intend to stay to hear any other talks; my schedule did not permit it. He told me that the place of the meeting was classified and, therefore, entrance to it required clearance. I replied that since it was the army that wanted me to be cleared, not me, the army should apply for my clearance, not me.

The officer then asked if I had ever been cleared by any military organization. I told him I had. He asked for details, which I provided. He then said he would get the information from the previous source of clearance, fill out the application form, and send it to me for my signature. I told him I would not sign it because doing so would make it my request for clearance, and it should be the army's. He assured me that the application had to have my signature. I said I would not provide it and again suggested he consult a good lawyer. Not surprisingly, the invitation to speak was withdrawn.

A few weeks later I was informed by telegram that I had been cleared to attend the meeting and asked if I would do so. I said I would. Again, no explanation for the change was provided.

> **MORAL: Clearance is not a way of clearing the way; it is a way of obstructing it.**

Laws, rules, and regulations are frequently misused. They are much more likely to be used as an excuse for not doing something than for doing it.

Systems and Dress

Bureaucratic systems try to deal with the unexpected in ways that preserve their images of reality and concepts of propriety.

🐭 🐭 🐭 **On Coding Dress at Work**

One day while working in my office at Case Institute of Technology, I received a phone call from the vice president of finance of the Chesapeake and Ohio (C&O) Railroad asking me to come to his company's headquarters at once. He wanted me to make a presentation to a board meeting that was already in progress. He wanted me to explain the approach we were taking to one of the railroad's major operating problems.

Although C&O's headquarters were less than half an hour away by car, I said I could not come immediately; I would have to go home and dress properly for the meeting. He said time was critical; dress was not. Therefore, I should come as I was. I explained that I was wearing a sweat suit and sneakers. Nevertheless, he insisted I come at once. I did. When I arrived on the executive floor I was immediately taken to the meeting in the boardroom.

Although I was on first-name terms with most of the members of the board, that day not one of them addressed me by my first name; they addressed me as "Professor Ackoff." It was apparent that doing so was their way of justifying my inappropriate dress.

> **MORAL: We tend to respect uniforms more than those who wear them.**

I learned something from this experience that has been useful to me ever since. There are times in my interactions with an organization's personnel when I want to be taken as one of them, and other times when I want to be kept distinct from them. I find that to a large extent I can control their perceptions of me by the way I dress. When I want to be perceived as one of them, I dress as one of them. When I want to be perceived as a university professor, I wear less formal clothing—but usually not a sweat suit; a sport coat and slacks does the trick.

I also learned that when corporate personnel come to my office for a working session, they like to dress informally, like university professors. It is a relief from their usual business attire, but more importantly it symbolizes a day devoted to thought rather than action. Whatever our reasons for informal dress in our offices, it is perfectly clear that it makes our visitors relax and feel more at home.

It is not surprising that the higher the tech of an organization —that is, the more thinking involved in its work—the less formally its members tend to dress. In addition, there has been a trend toward informal dress at work since the end of World War II. I suspect this is the product of both more permissive upbringing of the young and increased intellectual content of a good deal of white-collar work.

Dress obviously can be used as a way of symbolizing rank, as it is, for example, in the military. The need for such symbolism decreases the more that rank depends on competence and the more conspicuous that competence is.

Bureaucratic Errors

Bureaucracies seldom admit to making an error. My good friend Merrill Kilby took great delight in forcing them to own up to their mistakes. It took a great deal of creativity for him to succeed.

❦ ❦ ❦   Infallibility

For many years Merrill served as the administrative officer of the research group I directed in The Wharton School. He was one of the most dedicated antibureaucrats I have ever known. His antibureaucratic career within the university appeared to come to an end when he reached the age of compulsory retirement in the early 1980s. However, the Fates gave him one more shot at the university's bureaucracy.

Among the benefits due Merrill after his retirement was his full salary for three consecutive months. About six months after his retirement he appeared in my office and asked me to come with him to visit the university's benefits office. When I asked why, he said, "To have some fun." Knowing I would, I joined him.

When we appeared at the benefits office, a young woman came to the counter to help us. Merrill began by saying he had retired a few months earlier and that he was due his salary for three months after retirement, but that the university had made a mistake. At this point the woman interrupted and assured Merrill that the university does not make mistakes in administration of retirement benefits. Merrill said he was glad to hear that and asked if she would please put this in writing.

The request for a document took her by surprise and made her suspicious. She asked Merrill to wait while she consulted her supervisor. She left us for a few moments and returned with her supervisor in tow. He reiterated the infallibility of his office. Merrill said he did not doubt it, but he would like a letter to this effect so as to be absolved of responsibility for any error the university might have made.

At this point the supervisor also became suspicious and for the first time asked Merrill what he thought the university might have done incorrectly. Merrill then explained that he was continuing to receive monthly salary checks after the three that were due him. He produced the checks and showed them to the supervisor. The supervisor and the clerk were suitably embarrassed and apologized for their behavior. This, however, did not keep Merrill from rubbing it in a bit.

> **MORAL: The assumption of infallibility is best left to God, and He ought to think twice before making it.**

Antibureaucrats extract great satisfaction from cases in which bureaucracies cut off their noses to spite their faces. This occurs when they solve one problem in a way that creates another as bad as or worse than the first.

❦ ❦ ❦   *The Aborted Report*

The Case Institute of Technology research group of which I was a part had contracted with the Transportation Corps of the U.S. Army to study possible improvements in its vehicle-maintenance procedures. The contract required that, when the work was completed, a draft report be prepared and submitted to the contracting officer. He would circulate that report to responsible authorities and collect the changes they desired. These were then to be communicated to us for incorporation into the final version of the report.

Our research yielded an unexpected finding: The principal cause of failure of the types of equipment we studied was maintenance. This finding and its support were treated in detail in the draft report we submitted.

Coincidently, when our submission was made Congress was conducting hearings on the defense budget and was clearly looking for ways to reduce it. Officials in the Transportation Corps were worried when they saw our report because they thought it could be used by Congress to reduce the funds made available to the corps. Therefore, our report was classified as "secret." This deprived Congress of access to it, but, although this was not intended, it also deprived us of access to it. We could not prepare the required final version of the report because it was classified and we were not cleared to work with classified material at that time. The final version of that report never was prepared.

**MORAL: One is very likely to cut off one's own
nose when spiting another's face.**

On Turning Systems Inside Out

All of us tend to rationalize our unwillingness to do something by invoking restrictions or constraints that we imagine are imposed on us by a system that we cannot control. This process is seldom conscious and, therefore, is very difficult to correct. When another tries to do so, we resist, refusing to accept the fact that the constraints are self-imposed.

As part of a university's faculty I often proposed to its admin-istration some action for which there was no precedent. These proposals were almost always rejected with the explanation that they violated some rule or regulation. In such cases I always asked to see the relevant rule or regulation. It was very seldom produced. All sorts of excuses were used for this. The fact was that most of the alleged rules and regulations were fabrications of bureaucratic minds. After the alleged rule or regulation could not be produced, opposition to my proposals not only persisted but intensified, as though to punish me for claiming that there was a systemic deficiency. Rejection of my proposals continued to be attributed to externally imposed constraints.

Proposals and Propositioning

Bureaucracies are prone to forming habits, repetitive ways of doing things. For example, they usually require proposals from competitive suppliers of services that they, the bureaucracies, want to acquire. Laws or regulations frequently require that such proposals be submitted and that the choice of a supplier be based on them. Nevertheless, in my opinion, selecting a supplier on the basis of submitted proposals is about as rea-sonable as selecting an automobile on the basis of its manu-facturer's advertising.

Personally, I am unwilling to work for a client who selects a supplier on the basis of an unpaid-for proposal. Contrary to what may appear to be the case, my attitude toward proposals and those who act on them has not been a serious handicap in my consulting and research career. Quite the opposite: it has been responsible for some very important learning experiences. Here are a few of them:

🍏 🍏 🍏   *On Pro- and Con-Posals*

Back in my Case Institute days, I received a request for a proposal (an RFP) from a unit of the air force. It involved a study to determine how to communicate effectively in the presence of an intelligent source of noise. Translated, this meant: How do you communicate to someone when someone else is trying to prevent it? For example, how can an airplane's pilot and a ground controller communicate when an enemy is trying to jam their channel of communication?

The RFP went on to say that it wanted the researchers to use Game Theory in their quest for a solution. This struck me as ridiculous. I could see no possible connection between Game Theory and the communication problem. In my opinion, whoever wrote the RFP did not understand either Game Theory or communication. I wrote a letter to this effect to the relevant air force officer, using it to explain why we would not submit a proposal. I indicated very briefly what kinds of technology I thought were applicable to the problem.

Several weeks later I received a letter from the air force saying we had been awarded the contract on the strength of my letter. No proposal was required.

❦ ❦ ❦

It was a proposal of a very different color that brought the Ford Foundation and me together, briefly. I received a phone call from a vice president of the foundation, an old acquaintance, saying he had a project he would like to have us do for Ford. Two Middle East countries, traditional enemies, had agreed to a joint scientific effort directed at finding a peaceful solution to their differences. The vice president wanted us to facilitate and guide such an effort. I told him we were very much interested in doing so. "Fine," he said, "then prepare and submit a proposal to that effect."

I told him that his request made no sense. He had all the relevant information; we didn't. Therefore, why didn't he write the proposal he would like to receive, send it to us, and, after modifying it if necessary, we would sign and submit it to him. Much to my surprise, he agreed.

Several weeks later we received the proposal he had drafted. We made only a few minor changes, of which he approved. Then we signed and submitted the proposal. We heard nothing about it for about six months. Then we received a form letter from another vice president of the Ford Foundation thanking us for having submitted our proposal, but turning it down on the grounds that it did not fall into an area of current interest to the foundation.

❦ ❦ ❦

The danger of acting on the basis of a proposal was revealed to me in an incident involving the U.S. Department of the Interior. I received a request for a proposal from that department on a subject of great interest to me. The department wanted to determine how to locate facilities and services of the federal government so as to contribute to equalization of opportunity for (1) employment to minorities and (2) development to communities. The RFP specified the maximum amount that the government was willing to pay to have the work done. This amount struck me as ridiculously low. I did not see how the required work could possibly be done for that amount of money. Although I did not submit a proposal, I wrote to the department to this effect.

The contracting officer called me and we discussed my letter at length. He told me the department had received a number of proposals, all involving amounts no more than the maximum stated in the RFP. I told him that, in my opinion, those who submitted such proposals were either ignorant or deceitful. He did not agree, but we parted as friends.

About a year later he called me to say that a year earlier they had awarded the contract to a major consulting firm. He told me that the report it produced failed completely to address the problem the department had formulated. It addressed a lesser, not totally unrelated problem, that could be treated with the amount of resources made available. The contracting officer then told me he was sorry he had not taken my skepticism more seriously.

❦ ❦ ❦

I had a contrary experience with a request for a proposal issued by AT&T. When this company was deregulated and forced to break up, I was asked to submit a letter-length proposal for a study to determine *how the new AT&T should be organized. Since my research group had done a good deal of work for AT&T and several of its subsidiaries, the prospect of working on this very large and very complex problem was exciting to us. Because of this and the fact that only a letter-length proposal was required, I prepared one and submitted it.*

A short while later I received a phone call from one of the AT&T officials handling the matter. He told me he liked our proposal but his colleagues and company officials did not believe we could do what we said we would for the amount of money we quoted. He said the second-lowest bid they had received was several times larger than ours. Then he asked if we were sure we had estimated our cost correctly. I told him we were. He said he had to have a higher estimate of cost for the work we proposed in order to make it more believable to AT&T personnel. He asked if we would be willing to double it. I said no. The contract was awarded to someone else at eight times the cost we had estimated.

> **MORAL: It is better to put your money where your mouth is than to put it where someone else's mouth is.**

Contracts

Contracts are often as irrational as proposals and as obstructive to choice and development.

❦ ❦ ❦   *Pro- and Con-Tracting*

In the late 1950s I bought a plot in a heavily wooded rural area just outside Cleveland, Ohio. I then spent about six months in a labor of love, designing the house my wife and I wanted to build there. When the design was complete I gave it to four contractors for bids. While waiting for the bids, by sheer chance I was visited by a friend's father, John Rinkema, who was a retired building contractor from Chicago. He knew about my intention to build a house and asked if he could see my drawings. The two of us spent most of the evening going over them in detail. He suggested several valuable modifications.

John told me that of the many houses he had built, none had a design as modern as mine. He then said that his retirement bored him and that he would like to build my house. He asked if he could bid on it. I saw this as an opportunity to build my house under a rational contractual arrangement. In most building contracts, the contractor is paid a percentage of the total cost of the building, and is therefore motivated to make the building as expensive as possible. I wanted to put the contractor on my side, not against me.

When I explained my attitude toward building contracts to John, he was as interested as I in developing one that was sensible. After some discussion, John and I agreed that he would build the house for a price no greater than the lowest bid I received from the other contractors. In addition, he would calculate how much profit he would make on building the house at that price, and I would pay him that amount in advance. Subsequently, I would pay all bills. Finally, we agreed to divide equally each dollar less than the estimated cost for which he built the house.

This contract made the builder's interests and mine compatible. I wanted a reduction of my cost to be in his interest. It clearly turned out this way. John did a great job of building my house and he did so for $2,000 under the estimated cost. We split that saving.

❦ ❦ ❦

Not much later, my close friend and collaborator, C. West Churchman, who had moved to the San Francisco area about the time I built my house, bought land in Mill Valley and hired a young architect to design a house for him and his family. West gave the architect a set of carefully prepared specifications of the properties he wanted his house to have. Among these was a statement of the maximum price he was willing to pay for it.

I happened to visit West when he received the first design his architect had prepared. I examined the drawings carefully and told West that the house designed could not be built within the cost limits he had set.

West assured me that he had discussed cost with the architect and that the architect had assured him that the house could be built within his cost restriction. I could not convince West to the contrary. Shortly thereafter he put the design out for bids. The lowest bid he received was far above the upper limit he had set.

West was devastated. He and his wife had fallen in love with the architect's design, but they could not afford it. In order to reduce the cost of the house, features would have to be eliminated that they were now unwilling to give up. Therefore, when they went to work with the architect on reducing cost they never got it down to the originally stated maximum. West eventually built that house, but at a cost well above the maximum amount he had intended to spend.

> **MORAL: The principal objective of a contract should be to ensure terminal satisfaction of both parties.**

In my opinion, West's architect should not have been paid his fee. Architects are supposed to know the cost of building various types of structures, and they should adhere to a client's specification of a maximum expenditure. But since the architect's fee is usually a percentage of the total cost of the structure, it is in his or her interest to raise the cost of the structure as high as the client will go. The typical contract between client and architect puts the two in conflict.

The same type of conflict is apparent in contracts most corporations have with their advertising agencies. The agencies are paid a percentage of the amount their clients spend on advertising. This induces the agency to try to maximize its client's advertising expenditures; it is an agent to advertising media, not of its client.

Agencies need not be compensated in the traditional way. A number of years ago Anheuser-Busch established a very different kind of relationship with its agency, D'Arcy. D'Arcy's fee was set so that if the amount of advertising was reduced without a reduction of sales, or sales were increased without an increase in advertising, its fee would increase. However, if things went the other way, its fee would decrease.

Protection of the interests of the server, not the served, is the primary focus of most contracts for service. Those served usually do not know enough to ensure protection of their interests. This ignorance is exploited by servers who usually know more than enough to protect their interests.

Bureaucratic Monopolies

If development is to be accelerated in any social environment, many of the systems that it contains must be debureaucratized and demonopolized. The only way a bureaucratic monopoly can survive is to be subsidized, and to be subsidized in a way that is independent of its performance. This relieves it of any responsibility for effective service to those it is supposed to serve.

Government is full of such organizations, but so are corporations. Internal service units—for example, finance, personnel, research, and development units—are among those that in most corporations are bureaucratic monopolies. They are subsidized by a higher level unit, receive no financial support from their users, and their users have no alternative but to use their services. This situation constitutes a paradox.

We are committed to a market economy at the national (macro) level and to a nonmarket, centrally planned, hierarchically managed (micro) economy within most corporations and other types of organizations in our society. Our macro and micro economies are not consistent. They can be; market economies can be introduced within corporations and even government. In Chapter Two we will see how a market economy can work in the public school system by use of the voucher system.

Creation of a market economy within a firm requires that the following characteristics be designed into it.

1. Each unit in the organization, including the executive office, operates as a profit center.

2. Each unit also operates as an investment bank and government for its immediately subordinate units: It taxes their profits and receives payment (in the form of interest or dividends) for the capital it provides them. As a government, each unit can enact laws that preclude specified activities of subordinate units. For example, it may preclude outsourcing of products that involve a "secret" formula or production process. Such preclusions should be kept to a minimum.

3. Each unit is free either to supply itself with whatever goods and services it wants or to buy them internally or externally at a price acceptable to it. (This freedom is subject to an override, discussed in paragraph 6 below.)

4. Each unit is also free to sell its services or products internally or externally to whomever it wants at a price it establishes (subject to the same override).

5. Each unit can retain up to a specified amount of its profit for use as it sees fit. Any amount above this must be turned over to the next-higher level of management. In return, the unit is paid interest on this amount by the higher receiving unit.

6. Any manager can override a subordinate unit's decision to make, buy, or sell, but that manager must compensate that unit for any additional cost or loss of profit that it incurs because of that override.

The fact that every unit operates as a profit center does not imply that its principal objective is to maximize annual profit or return on investment. What is implied is that profitability be taken into account in evaluating each unit's performance, but this need not be annual profitability. Nor does this requirement imply that every unit must be profitable. An organization may maintain an unprofitable unit for nonfinancial reasons—for example, for the prestige it brings. Nevertheless, repeatedly unprofitable units should be reviewed periodically for possible discontinuation or divestment.

Note that this type of internal economy eliminates subsidized monopolies operating within an organization. All internal units that supply goods or services and for which there are alternative external sources of supply must compete with them even for internal business. This makes them more responsive and efficient suppliers.

An internal market economy is as applicable to a not-for-profit or governmental organization as it is to one for profit. Even though an organization as a whole is subsidized by an external source, it can distribute funds internally solely for services rendered or products supplied. For example, as I mentioned earlier, students can be given freedom to choose their schools, and the income of publicly supported schools can be restricted to a payment for each student enrolled.

Conclusion

Beating a system that obstructs or constrains development is a challenge. Succeeding is fun. It brings with it the joy of victory over a huge, impersonal, and inflexible machine-like mind. Beating a system is a creative act, like solving a puzzle or designing something new. It involves overcoming self-imposed constraints. Trying to beat a system requires exercise of all the mental functions: thinking, sensing, feeling, and intuition. It contrasts with passive acceptance of what is. It occupies our mind with what might be, imagining a future that would be better than the present.

Significant personal and cultural development is not possible without beating systems. In some cases, systems are beaten, even destroyed, by use of force. However, it is much better to beat them by use of ideas. Force is directed at getting rid of what we don't want; ideas are directed at getting what we do want. They are not equivalent: getting rid of what we don't want does not assure us of getting what we want. For example, changing TV channels to get rid of a program we don't want does not assure us of getting a program we do want.

When we beat a system, we make it do something it did not intend to do and, in the case of a bureaucratic system, something it proscribed. Beating a system not only removes constraints imposed on us by the system, but also removes constraints imposed on the system by itself. This extends its range of choices and enables it to develop. Without choice there are no mistakes; without mistakes there is no learning, and without learning there is no development.

Most systems, like recalcitrant children, do not appreciate being beaten, even when the beating is good for them. This is especially true of bureaucracies. They find choice unsettling; they prefer a static equilibrium produced by complete conformity to rule in an unchanging environment: continuous repetition of the expected. Whatever else creativity implies, it implies production of the unexpected. It is the unexpected that produces the quantum leaps in development and quality of life.

Chapter Two

Rubbish Heaps Grow, but They Don't Develop

Understanding the Differences between Growth and Development

❦ ❦ ❦

The dinosaur's eloquent lesson is that if some bigness is good, an overabundance of bigness is not necessarily better.

—Eric A. Johnston

❦ ❦ ❦   *A Little Grass Shack*

Close to the end of the World War II campaign on the island of Leyte in the Philippines, I was doing reconnaissance for the engineering section of X Corps Headquarters. My work involved looking for natural materials that could be used in construction projects. I did this while traveling with one of the infantry divisions attached to the corps. Each day I transmitted my findings back to corps headquarters by phone.

One morning when I phoned headquarters I was told to return as soon as possible; the commanding general of the corps wanted to see me. This sounded ominous; I had never been sent for by a general. Since I was only a sergeant at the time, I was sure the summons meant trouble; it was easy to think of possible reasons for my being in it.

I worked my way back from the western to the eastern side of the island, where headquarters was located. I arrived there too late to report to the general. I reported first thing in the morning. When I was shown into his office, he put me at ease and told me to sit down. Consulting the content of a large file folder on his desk, he said, "I see by the records that you have a degree in architecture. Is that right?"

I said it was.

He then asked if I had ever practiced architecture before coming into the army. When I said I had, he questioned me in detail about the firm I had worked for and the types of buildings I had designed. He then asked if I had ever done any architecture in the army. I told him I had spent more than a year doing architectural work in the Desert Training Center in Southern California. He asked detailed questions about this work.

After I replied, he closed my personnel file, sat back, and said, "You might do."

He went on to explain. "The fighting on this island is almost over. We've had a very hard few months. The men are worn out and need a rest. I want to build a recreation center that can accommodate several hundred soldiers at a time. I'm looking for someone to design it and supervise its construction. Can you do it and are you interested?"

This was equivalent to inviting me to leave hell and enter heaven. Of course I was interested. He told me he had selected a site he would like to show me. We left his office and took a short ride in an LCI (Landing Craft Infantry) around the top of the island until we came to Barugo, a small town at the mouth of a river of the same name. We went down the river about a mile and pulled up against its east bank. This bank formed the edge of a large, grass-covered plateau that was surrounded by woods. The site was perfect for a recreational center. I said this to the general after going over it thoroughly. He was satisfied and we left.

On the way back, he told me to get started the following day. I asked him how many engineers would be assigned to help me build the center. He looked at me with surprise and said he had none to spare; they were still needed for combat-related missions. Then I was surprised; I asked him who would help with the construction. He said he would provide me with enough funds to hire about 150 natives. I pointed out that I could not speak their language. He told me that an interpreter would be provided. When I remarked that the natives might not be skilled enough to be helpful, he said, "Then train them." I expressed some doubt about my ability to do so but hastened to point out that I was very willing to try.

Then I asked what construction materials and equipment would be available for the job. Again the general expressed surprise; he said he had none to spare. He told me to find out what materials the natives used and use them. This did not strike me as the best possible way of going about it, but going about it any way was better than returning to the combat zone.

I started work the following day. Equipped with an interpreter, I went to the village of Barugo and asked to speak to the best builder in town. I was told that the best builders were two brothers. I asked to see them. One of the villagers went off and fetched them. Surrounded by a large number of the villagers, I asked the builders if they would build a house for me. They showed some doubt about my sanity. The tents at headquarters were superior to the one-room shacks in which they lived. They asked why I wanted a house. I explained that I didn't, but that I wanted to see what they used to build it with and how they did it. They asked what I would do with the house after it was completed. I told them they could keep it. That settled it; they signed on and began work the following morning.

For the next few days I watched closely as they built a typical shack. It was built up off the ground, on posts formed by trunks of coconut palms. The shack itself was built of bamboo and nipa, a long grass, which the natives wove around a piece of bamboo to form a large shingle or mat. These shingles were attached to bamboo framing to cover the walls and the roof. The framing was formed by bamboo rods tied together by nipa. No materials other than the trunks of coconut palms, bamboo, and nipa were used.

When the house was completed I went to the drawing board and started to design the center. Two major design problems confronted me. The first derived from the fact that the Barugo River, which was ideal for swimming, rose and fell several feet with the tide. At low tide the river was too far below the bank and too shallow to dive into for swimming. At high tide it was fine. Therefore, I had to build a dock that would extend out into the river far enough to reach deep water at low tide, would rise and fall with the tide, and would hold at least a hundred men. What material could I make it out of? The coconut palm trunks were too heavy and dense to float. I needed something more buoyant.

I solved the dock problem by using empty 55-gallon drums that were strewn around the island. I was able to build a cage and floor of bamboo and enclose a large number of drums within that cage. This produced a floating dock. Then I built a hinged ramp from the bank to the dock. It rose and fell with the tide and the dock. The dock rode up and down with the tide on vertical poles formed by trunks of coconut palms driven down into the river bed.

The second design problem arose from the fact that all the native shacks leaned away from the prevailing wind. The grass that was used to bind pieces of bamboo together stretched when the humidity rose. If this occurred when there was a wind, the shack leaned in the direction of the wind. I didn't want the buildings in the recreation center to do the same. This problem was solved by using another material liberally sprinkled over the island: Signal Corps wire. With help from the natives I found a way of tying two pieces of bamboo together with wire so as to obtain a rigid joint.

Thus equipped and supplied, the natives and I built a recreational center that had playing fields for major sports; a large enclosed space for dressing, undressing, and taking a shower (with water held in more of the 55-gallon drums); a large enclosed space for indoor sports; and the swimming dock.

During construction, the number of natives in the audience increased each day. They were generous with their advice and kept assuring me that we would not be able to do things that we did. After the center was completed, dedicated, and opened, a number of the natives of

Barugo who had worked on the project tore down their homes and rebuilt them using what they had learned while building the recreation center. What surprised the natives most was that I had used only materials and tools readily available to them, but I had used these materials and tools in ways that had not occurred to them.

MORAL: Development is not a matter of how much one has, but of how much one can do with whatever one has.

The Nature of Development

There are few concepts as widely misunderstood as development. It is usually taken to have the same meaning as growth, but neither growth nor development is necessary for the other. One can grow without developing and develop without growing. People grow when they get larger. Some who are seriously retarded grow without developing. On the other hand, many adults continue to develop long after they have stopped growing—in fact, even as they are contracting due to old age.

Growth is an increase in size or number. Development is not as easy to define.

To develop is to increase one's desire and ability to satisfy one's own legitimate needs and desires, and those of others. A legitimate need or desire is one that, when satisfied, does not deprive others of the opportunity to satisfy their legitimate needs and desires. A need is what is required for health or survival—for example, food and oxygen. What is needed may not be desired; an individual may need calcium but, being unaware of the need, not desire it. On the other hand, people have been known to desire what they do not need.

Development has to do with mental properties; growth, with physical properties.

The Four Aspects of Development

The continuous pursuit of development has four interacting aspects: the scientific-technological, the economic, the ethical-moral, and the aesthetic.

First, continuous development requires continuous improvement of the means we employ in pursuit of our ends; that is, increases in their efficiency. Increases in the efficiency of available means are consequences of the discovery of truth by science and its practical application by technology. Scientific and technological progress, a product of research and development, has been so apparent in the developed nations of the West that it is taken for granted as obvious. The speed at which we can travel and communicate, for example, has increased more in my lifetime than it had in all of history prior to my birth.

Dissemination of information about the availability and use of newly developed and more efficient means is one of the principal functions of our educational institutions.

Second, means are courses of action that frequently require the use of resources: equipment and facilities, materials, energy, services, money, and information. Plenty is the state of abundance of resources, a state symbolized by the ancient Greeks as a self-replenishing cornucopia. It is the function of society's economic institutions to pursue such abundance. The standard of living is the most commonly used measure of the extent to which they have succeeded.

The amount of wealth we have is the amount of resources we have available for use. Therefore, the function of economic institutions, put another way, is to produce, distribute, protect, and maintain wealth. Business and industry are primarily occupied with the production and distribution of wealth. The maintenance and security of our resources is the responsibility of some businesses and industries—insurance, for example, and equipment maintenance and repair—but also of such institutions as the police, the military, environmental protection agencies, the health system, and so on.

There is little disagreement over the assertion that developed Western societies have made significant economic progress at least since the Industrial Revolution.

Third, two needs and/or desires are in conflict if the attainment of one necessarily involves the failure to obtain the other. Therefore, an increase in one's ability to obtain one of a conflicting pair of objectives necessarily involves a decrease in the ability to obtain the other. Put another way: if an individual has conflicting objectives that person cannot continuously increase his or her ability to obtain all of them, and if different individuals have conflicting objectives each of them cannot simultaneously increase their ability to obtain these objectives. The reduction of such conflicts is the function of institutions devoted to promoting ethics and morality, pursuit of the good. The church and the United Nations function as such institutions; psychiatry focuses on reduction of internal conflict (within individuals) and labor arbitrators focus on reduction of external conflict (between individuals).

The objective of reducing conflict between individuals and groups is peace on Earth; within individuals and groups it is peace of mind. Some people argue that Western societies have made some progress toward these ends over their histories: that they are more humane and more concerned with reduction of intra-societal conflict as reflected in their efforts to provide an equitable distribution of opportunity and wealth. Many, of course, would deny this.

The fourth aspect of development, aesthetics, has to do with the recreative and creative aspects of ideal pursuit, the derivation of fun and inspiration from what we do. Fun is the product of recreational activities such as play and entertainment. It is the satisfaction we derive from what we do independently of why we do it. Recreation provides the pauses that refresh in the pursuit of the developmental and other ideals which, by their very nature, are unattainable. Without such intermediate payoffs, pursuit of ideals would not be sustainable. Continuous pursuit of any ideal also requires a vision of something more desirable than our current state. It also requires the courage to pursue it—the willingness to make short-term sacrifices for longer-term progress. Beauty, natural or manmade (which is art), inspires us to formulate and pursue ideals; it is a source of the drive to create a new and better life.

The satisfaction derived from what we do independently of why we do it, and the satisfaction we derive from behavior that moves us toward meaningful ideals, are the two essential ingredients of quality of life. Therefore, quality of life is primarily a matter of aesthetics; standard of living is primarily a matter of economics.

Because development involves an increase in ability, it empowers, but only in a particular way: It increases *power-to*, not *power-over*. Power-over is authority, and authority is the ability to make someone do something he does not want to do, usually by threat of punishment. Therefore, to exercise power over others is to reduce their ability to satisfy their needs and desires. Power-to is the ability to implement decisions. This type of power increases with competence, hence development. In the ideal state, everyone would be able to get whatever he or she legitimately needed or wanted without the exercise of power-over. In states short of the ideal, politics has to do with the distribution of power-over. The political ideal, then, is a state in which no one has power over another but all have unlimited power-to. The ideal state is one in which there is no need for politics.

As noted above, those who are fortunate enough to have been born and raised in a developed nation believe that at least part of mankind has made significant scientific and economic progress. Whether or not ethical-moral progress has been made is still being debated, but at least some think it has. However, practically no one believes the Western world has made aesthetic progress. Few if any believe that we can produce more or better beauty and fun, or that we can appreciate them more than our ancestors. Recognition of this lack of aesthetic progress in the Western world has led to our current preoccupation with a deteriorating quality of life and our increasing willingness to sacrifice some of our standard of living to improve that quality.

Development and Quality of Life

How much one has determines one's standard of living; how much one can do with what one has determines one's quality of life. Therefore, quality of life is a better indicator of development than is standard of living. Standard of living is an indicator of growth, not development.

This does not mean that how much one has (wealth) is irrelevant to one's quality of life. The quality of life that one can realize depends on the amount and kind of resources available and one's level of development. Although a well-developed person can do more than a less-developed person with the same resources, the more resources available, the better the quality of life that can be realized by people at any level of development. Development is a potential for improving quality of life, not the quality of life actually obtained.

Resources are created by people out of what nature provides. The more developed a person, the more resources he or she can create from whatever nature provides, and therefore the less dependent that person is on resources made available by others.

Development and Learning

Development is a matter of learning, not earning, and learning is a matter of education. Therefore, education is the process by which development takes place. Because learning is the essence of development, and because one person cannot learn for another, no one can develop another. There is only one kind of development: self-development. But one person or institution can encourage and facilitate the development of others. The encouragement and facilitation of personal development is the most important function of education.

Although education requires learning, learning does not require teaching. For example, most of us learned our first language without it having been taught to us. We learned it through experience. Few who have been taught a second language learn it as well as they learned their first. Most of what we need to know at work and play we learn at work and play, not in school from a teacher. No wonder the aphorism: *Experience is the best teacher.*

Therefore, although learning is necessary for development, being taught is not. For this reason, many who are relatively untutored are nevertheless remarkably developed.

❦ ❦ ❦   *All Mantua is Divided into Seven Parts*

Since the late 1960s I have been working with a group of people from Mantua, one of Philadelphia's so-called urban black ghettos, on their neighborhood's self-development effort. The neighborhood occupies about 80 city blocks and contains a little more than 20,000 people. It was once commonly referred to as "The Bottom." This said more about it than all the descriptive statistics put together.

In the early 1970s the city's school board announced that it intended to build a new middle school (junior high) on the northern edge of the neighborhood. Shortly thereafter, four Mantuans came to my office in the Wharton School to ask for help in stopping construction of the proposed school. I was surprised by their request because Mantuans had frequently told me how much their neighborhood needed new schools. Why, I asked, did they want to block the new school? Doris Hamilton, one of the group, answered by asking me if I had to have an answer before I would help them. I said no, but it would be very difficult to help them without knowing why I was doing so. Furthermore, I asked, why was she hesitant to give me an explanation? She said that I didn't know enough about ghetto life for the explanation to make any sense to me. I said that although this might well be true, I would never become very helpful to the community unless I gained such understanding.

Doris gave a sigh of resignation and went to the blackboard in my office. She drew a rough map of Mantua and then divided it into parts. She said, "All Mantua is divided into seven turfs." I asked what she meant by "turf." That, she said, is what it would be hard for her to explain and for me to understand. Again I asked her to try.

A turf, she said, is the territory claimed by a neighborhood gang. It was dangerous for a boy 12 years old or more to walk alone in a turf other than the one in which he lived; if he did, he was likely to be attacked by the gang that claimed that turf. Therefore, membership in a gang became virtually compulsory for males of that age because it enabled them to walk through foreign turfs in groups. Even so, violent conflict often resulted. About a dozen young men had been killed in gang fights during the previous year. A much larger number had been injured and hospitalized, and a number of innocent bystanders had also been hurt. Furthermore, an eligible male who did not join the gang in his own turf was in danger of attack when he walked through even that turf.

Doris pointed out that the location of the proposed school would require young men in the relevant age group to pass through a number of hostile turfs on their way to and from school. She said that because of *the danger such passage would involve, many would avoid it by playing hooky or dropping out of school.*

I told Doris that I thought I understood her explanation. But, I said, if Mantuans wanted to stop the proposed school, it would help if they had an alternative to propose to the school board. She said that they had one but they doubted that the school board would consider it seriously, because it was so unconventional. When I asked what that alternative was, she said the Mantuans wanted a new primary rather than middle school, each classroom of which would be located in a different turf. She called this dispersed school the Scatter School. Students would then be required to go to a different classroom each day. This meant that young boys, not yet of gang age, would repeatedly walk through all the turfs in their neighborhood while they were still free to do so. Such movement, Doris said, would give them a sense of neighborhood that might dominate their sense of turf. If it did, the gang structure of Mantua would weaken, and this, she said, was what they wanted to happen.

The Scatter School struck me as a great idea, more sophisticated, creative, and pragmatic than anything I had heard suggested by so-called educational experts. However, I pointed out that such a school would cost a great deal more to build than one that was conventional. The neighborhood planners agreed. However, they asked if it would be possible to build more than one primary school building at no more cost to the city than that of the proposed middle school.

We subsequently learned from the school board how much the proposed middle school would cost. Once we knew this, we were able to determine that we could build a three-part Scatter School for the cost to the city of building the proposed middle school. We then determined where the three parts of the school should be located. Analysis revealed the three locations that would require school attendees to pass through the largest average number of turfs per week.

The Scatter School concept was implemented; over the next few years it contributed significantly to the elimination of gangs in Mantua.

MORAL: Intelligence and creativity are producers,
not products, of education, but they are often its
victims.

Education and Schooling

Recall that development is more a matter of learning than of
earning, and learning is obviously a matter of education. What
is not so obvious is that education is not necessarily a matter
of schooling. One can get an education without going to school
and one can go to school without getting an education. Nevertheless, schools are supposed to educate and to some degree
they do, but this degree has been decreasing over several recent
decades. As a result, schools have been severely criticized by
a number of prominent educators. Here is a sample of such
criticism:

> It is not possible to spend any prolonged period visiting public
> school classrooms without being appalled by the mutilation vis-
> ible everywhere—mutilation of spontaneity, of joy of learning,
> of pleasure in creating, of sense of self. . . . Because adults take
> schools so much for granted, they fail to appreciate what grim,
> joyless places most American schools are, how oppressive and
> petty are the rules by which they are governed, how intellec-
> tually sterile and esthetically barren the atmosphere, what an
> appalling lack of civility obtains on the part of teachers and
> principals, what contempt they unconsciously display for chil-
> dren.[1]

> If their parents do not see that they go to school, the parents
> may be judged unfit and the kids go to jail. . . . No matter how
> bad school is, it is better than jail. Everyone knows that, and
> the schools know it especially.[2]

> The pupil is . . . "schooled" to confuse teaching with learning,
> grade advancement with education, a diploma with competence,
> and fluency with the ability to say something new. His imagi-
> nation is "schooled" to accept service in place of value. . . .[3]

Piecemeal reform and concessions to student pressure, most educational experts agree, will not be sufficient. What is needed is a frontal assault on the existing school structure that will replace outmoded teaching methods, impersonal or authoritarian teacher-student relations and obsolete behavior codes with new forms and ideas more in tune with the times.[4]

Our nation is at risk. Our once-unchallenged preeminence in commerce, industry, science, and technological innovation is being overtaken by competitors throughout the world. . . . We report to the American people that . . . the educational foundations of our society are presently being eroded by a rising tide of mediocrity that threatens our very future as a nation and people.[5]

. . . the public school system's performance would have been disappointing even if educational standards had remained serenely stable. . . . Corrected for inflation, annual current expenditures per pupil attending public schools had been the equivalent of $478 in 1920–30, was about $1,123 in 1958, and would become $2,670 by 1981–82. . . . Teacher productivity, as measured by the number of pupils per teacher, fell steadily until 1970 and then stabilized at around 20 pupils per teacher. The problem in recent years has been a proliferation of school bureaucracy. The number of pupils per administrator had dropped from 523 in 1948–50 to 295 in 1979–80.[6]

Colleges and universities, as well as lower-grade public schools, have come under attack. However, almost all these attacks incorrectly assume that the principal objective of institutions of higher learning is the one they proclaim: education of students. Having spent my entire adult life in such institutions, it has become apparent to me that this is not the case; their principal objective is to maximize the quality of work lives of their faculties. Teaching is a price faculties must pay to get the quality of work life they want; as with all prices, they try to minimize it.

I was once appointed to represent The Wharton School on the faculty of another college of the University of Pennsylvania. For two years I attended every faculty meeting of that college. Since I was bored stiff by the proceedings, I accumulated statistics about their content. The word "student" was only mentioned once in the two-year period.

In the field of management, with which I have been most closely associated, students are equipped with a vocabulary that enables them to speak authoritatively about subjects they do not understand and to accept principles that have demonstrated their ability to withstand any amount of disconfirming evidence.

> Managers are not taught in formal education programs what they most need to know to build successful careers in management. Unless they acquire through their own experience the knowledge and skills that are vital to their effectiveness, they are not likely to advance up the organizational ladder.
>
> Although an implicit objective of all formal management education is to assist managers to learn from their own experience, much management education is, in fact, miseducation because it arrests or destroys the ability of managerial aspirants to grow as they gain experience. Fast learners in the classroom often, therefore, become slow learners in the executive suite.[7]

Because of such criticism as I have cited here, the educational system has repeatedly been said to be in a "state of crisis." Such a statement seems inappropriate to me, because a crisis is usually taken to be a situation in which, unless decisive action is taken quickly, dire consequences will follow rapidly. Crises are turning points in which significant qualitative changes of state are likely to occur unless a significant change is made in the individual or organization involved. No such changes have been made in the educational system, yet it survives and continues to deteriorate unabated.

The educational system has demonstrated an unlimited ability to resist responding to any of its problems. When it does respond, it does so like a coiled spring, modifying itself as little as necessary to accommodate the pressure being applied to it, and returning to its original state as soon as the pressure is removed.

> . . . established social systems have the advantage; they are able to exert continuing energy in the service of their stable state, whereas those attacking can seldom sustain their attack.[8]

Demonopolization and Debureaucratization of Schools

The need for changes in the educational system—not necessarily the ones I have suggested—has long been recognized. Nevertheless, this system has not changed fundamentally in more than a century. Educational administrators and planners are unable to let go of old models and concepts. Worse yet, they tend to be satisfied with the fundamental characteristics of the existing system and restrict their changes to nonessential characteristics of that system.

Most educators blame the plight of education on the family, the public, politicians, and everything else in sight other than themselves. They believe that, whatever the deficiencies of the system, they can be overcome with the infusion of more money. The quality of education is believed to be directly proportional to the amount spent on education per student per year and the number of years over which it is spent. Thus, quality of education is taken to be directly proportional to the quantity of resources consumed by it. This is a terrible distortion of the meaning of quality. There is no necessary connection between the quality of education and the quantity of resources it consumes. In addition, the continuous call for more resources completely ignores considerations of productivity:

Leaving quality questions aside, [U.S.] public school productivity, measured by number of employees required to process a
given number of students, seems to have declined by 46 percent
between 1957 and 1979. Even the poor old steel industry managed to increase its output per worker-hour 36 percent during
this period. Overall business sector productivity rose 65 percent.[9]

To the best of my knowledge no one has argued that the quality
of education improved over the same 20 years.

What is required is an educational system that is ready, willing,
and able to change, to experiment with new pedagogy, new
educational content, new organization of that content, and new
designs of the facilities and equipment used. In order to get
there, the current educational system must be debureaucratized
and demonopolized:

> The problems of education are . . . the problems typical of any
> socialized monopoly. . . . Symptoms include: the persistent ten-
> dency . . . to treat capital as a free good and all possible uses of
> it as equal; constant mismatching of supply and demand . . . ;
> prices administered without regard to incentives . . . ; an ab-
> sence of internal checks and balances to prevent wholesale im-
> position of officially favored enthusiasms . . . ; a pervasive
> politicization; a search for panaceas; and inexorable growth.[10]

In addition, if the educational system is to be improved significantly, its stakeholders must be given an opportunity to
participate in its redesign and administration.

Most institutional and organizational development derives
from (1) the need to compete for customers who have alternative sources of supply of the goods or services the institution
or organization provides, and (2) the fact that payment for
services made *by customers* is the principal, if not the only,
source of income to the provider. Neither of these conditions
is met by public schools. Most students and their parents have

no choice of school; they are assigned to one that is subsidized, and its subsidy is relatively independent of the quality, if not the quantity, of service it renders. Therefore, most public schools are monopolies within the areas of responsibility assigned to them. (Private schools are not an option to most students for financial, religious, or geographic reasons.)

In addition, because the survival of schools depends more on satisfying their subsidizers than on satisfying their users, they tend toward bureaucracy. Bureaucracies tend to grow indefinitely, because they believe that the larger they are, the less likely they are to be disposed of. They usually grow by creating make-work—work that keeps people busy doing nothing, that has no useful product. However, make-work often keeps those who have real work to do from doing it effectively.

The demonopolization and debureaucratization of public schools can be accomplished by providing students and/or their parents with a choice of schools and making the income of schools depend on the number of students they serve. The voucher system, first formulated by Jenks,[11] does these things. What follows is my own variation on his theme.

The parents of each school-age child would be given an educational voucher worth a specified amount of money payable by the government to the school that receives it. This voucher would cover tuition and transportation (if required) to any public school, or part or all of tuition to a private school. The choice of school would lie with students and/or their parents.

Schools that have more applicants than they can accommodate would be required to select from among them in the following way: First, they would have to accept applicants who live within their designated areas of responsibility. If there are more such applicants than they can accommodate, they would select from among them at random. If there are fewer such applicants than they can accommodate, they would select randomly from among applicants who reside outside their designated areas.

Public schools would have no source of income other than that obtained by redeeming the vouchers received from students they admit. If a school's costs exceeded its income, it might well be allowed to go out of business.

Private schools would be permitted to accept and redeem vouchers only if they selected new applicants at random. They would be able to charge whatever they wanted, but parents or guardians would have to cover any charges in excess of the value of the voucher. These conditions would create competition between public and private schools, as well as among public schools.

The voucher system would encourage differences among schools. Needed specialization would take place. For example, if there were a large number of retarded children requiring education, schools would specialize in serving them, particularly if their vouchers had a higher redemption value, as they might well have.

Moreover, the voucher system would eliminate involuntarily segregated schools, since students and/or their parents would have a choice of schools to which to apply, and the students' chances of being selected would be independent of their race or any other personal characteristics. This follows from the requirement that students be admitted by random selection from among the applicants.

By introducing the market mechanism into the educational system—as the voucher system does—parents, guardians, and children would be encouraged to become familiar with the schools available to them. Each community should provide a clearinghouse of information about schools, including evaluations of them by children and parents as well as educators.

In the voucher system, schools would experience relatively rapid feedback on their performance, hence learn more than they do now from their successes and failures. They would also become more adaptive and more responsive to the needs and desires of students, parents, guardians, other stakeholders, and the communities of which they are a part. School administrators would be more likely to try to involve their stakeholders in planning and policymaking. This would encourage and facilitate the personal development of the participants as well as make the schools more responsive to those they serve.

Participative Education

Suppliers of a service such as education who are not subject to control by those served (students and their parents or guardians) often assume they are infallible. This assumption deprives them of the ability to think creatively about their services or to learn from those who do so. Most educators believe that laymen cannot contribute to improvement of institutionalized education. This is nonsense.

There is widespread realization that the process of development can be very much accelerated by prompting the participation of the concerned people on both designing and implementing such activities. An educational activity designed to promote such participation cannot itself be conducted in a nonparticipative way. The traditional way of imparting education to children, in which the teacher talks and others listen, will not be conducive to education of the adults. This itself has to become participative, in which the learners become active partners in the process of educating themselves. Newer educational methods are obviously needed here. The process and methods of education cannot be separated from the intended content and objectives of education, particularly in the context of development activities. It is becoming increasingly clear that the concerned rural poor themselves have to play an active role both in their education and in their development. The adult educators and others involved in such activities can play, at best, the role of facilitators of this process and as resource persons for various content inputs. Participation in the process of education is vital even when functional literacy is involved, because even simple literacy cannot be separated from the life problems of the learners—in this case the rural poor. The more they become aware of the deeper socioeconomic problems and develop readiness for confronting such problems, the more motivated they become to take part in educational activities, including functional literacy.[12]

Many of even those educators who accept adult involvement in educational design argue that children are not competent to participate. There are many experiments that refute this—for example, the Gruppo Futuro and similar experiments in Naples, Italy, and Oxford, England.

> Our intention was to try to create a procedure (process) in which children could actively experiment with as many media as possible in order to express, propose, question, and build alternative futures with minimal interference/domination from adults (especially those likely to specialize and profess). . . .
>
> Our role became that of providing an initial spark of an idea that change and different futures are possible. We found that most of the children already knew this but that schooling prohibited thoughts about many kinds of change, especially a change not of a scientific or technological nature. We became not only facilitators, but intervened in the school setting.
>
> This "intervention" consisted of handing over communication tools to the children. . . . The intervention also consisted of creating an environment where change is acceptable; most often the changes expressed by the children had to do with community, feelings, and institutions.[13]

Participation in design of the educational process by its stake-holders would ensure the relevance of the education provided. For example, students in rural areas would probably learn how to engage more productively in agricultural activities. Their education would not force them to migrate to cities to find employment to which their education could be applied.

Participative design and administration of the educational pro-cess would expand rather than contract the horizons of children and adults. It would unify work, play, and learning, rectifying the harm done by societies that isolate each of these activities. It is only by making life whole (for children as well as for adults) that work, play, and learning can be engaged in satisfactorily and developmentally.

Continuing Education

The need for education was once thought to end when a person reached maturity. This is no longer the case. People of all ages turn to education either to increase their relevance at work or to enrich their lives. We now take for granted the need for continued or lifelong education.

As Mehta noted, the form and content of education must change with age. Educational institutions are not able to treat adults as badly as children. In addition, adult education has little history. Therefore, it offers more opportunities for inno-vation and experimentation, particularly because more of it is offered by corporations than by educational institutions. Recent studies show that corporations collectively are spending more on education than all the institutions of higher learning put together.

Although the opportunities for educational innovation and ex-perimentation are considerable, most offerings to adults, including those provided by corporations, tend to be very conservative in both form and content. Most courses directed at raising skill levels of adults are modeled on graduate courses offered by institutions of higher learning. In fact, many are given by faculty of these institutions as an extracurricular and income-generating activity on or off campus. Most courses directed at broadening the perspectives of adults, increasing their understanding of what is going on in their environments, or enriching their work or social lives, are an academic vaudeville show. One speaker after another puts on his act independently of the others, and most of them are more concerned with entertaining than educating their audiences. Course designers and administrators try to sequence these presentations so there is some semblance of structure, but most of the resulting structure is apparent only to them, not to the students.

Obstructions to Development

Older students are easier to teach than younger ones in some respects. Their richer experiential backgrounds enable them to grasp and understand thoughts and ideas that evade younger students. On the other hand, their minds are more difficult to change. They have many more defenses against innovation. They are less inclined to make the effort required to unlearn what they think they know, and they have a lot more to unlearn. And they imagine they know a lot more than they do.

☕ ☕ ☕   *On Prenatal Failures*

I was working with a group of directors of a major railroad early in the 1950s when they raised questions about the effective operation of a classification yard. I pointed out that a recently developed mathematical technique called linear programming was capable of improving these operations significantly. It could be used to answer most of the questions the directors had raised. The managers asked me to describe the technique. Reducing it to ordinary English was not easy, but I tried.

Throughout my presentation the oldest member of the company's board fiddled with his hearing aid. I found this very distracting, although I could not tell whether he was tuning me in or out.

When I completed my explanation of linear programming a number of questions were asked. After a little time, the oldest member of the board cleared his throat, thereby announcing his intention to say something. The room quieted down.

He said, "Young man (his eyesight also left something to be desired), I didn't hear half of what you said. Most of what I did hear I could not understand. But we've been doing that stuff for at least 20 years, and it doesn't work."

MORAL: There is no such thing as a new trick to an old dog.

The presentation of a new idea often provokes requests for examples of its successful application and identification of some who have used it. Once an example is provided, the one who requested it is almost certain to point out that the organization involved in the successful application is significantly different from the one of which he/she is a member, the implication being: The idea does not apply to me or my organization. I have found it futile to point out to such people that no two organizations are identical but not all their differences are relevant when it comes to implementation of a new idea. Older students are more likely than younger ones to focus on non-essential differences rather than essential similarities.

Most adults tend to underestimate how much their juniors know. Those who underestimate their juniors almost always underestimate their seniors as well. I have found that most people in positions of authority doubt that any of their subordinates can do their jobs as well as they do, but the same people believe they can do their boss's job at least as well as he or she can. Underestimation of the ability of subordinates is magnified when the subordinates lack the formal education their superiors have. No one overestimates the educational value of advanced formal education as much as one who has been subjected to it. Such people tend to confuse the contributions of such education to their incomes with its contribution to their minds. Advanced education often increases one's earning power without increasing one's knowledge or understanding. It provides a license for charging more.

There are other ways of rationalizing the unwillingness to pay attention to younger people or new ideas.

❦ ❦ ❦   *I've Been Working on the Railroad*

In recent years, corporate culture has become the focus of increasing attention. I first became aware of it on the very first industrial project on which I participated. In 1951, the operations research group at what was then Case Institute of Technology in Cleveland began work for the major railroad previously referred to. Early in the project I had my first meeting with that railroad's board. During that meeting one member of the board asked me if I had ever worked on a railroad. I told him I hadn't. He then asked if my father had ever worked on a railroad. Again I said, "No."

"Has anyone in your family ever worked on a railroad?"

Once again I had to say, "No."

"Then how," he asked, "can you expect to be able to help this railroad solve any of its problems?"

> **MORAL: A one-track mind cannot effectively
> manage a two-track railroad.**

In reply to the railroader's question, I told him a story I had heard as an architectural student. It was a story I could not authenticate, but it was good enough to be true. It involved the great architect Frank Lloyd Wright and the distinguished architectural critic Louis Mumford.

❦ ❦ ❦   *Which Goose Laid Which Egg?*

*When Frank Lloyd Wright's Guggenheim Museum in New York City
had been completed, Louis Mumford wrote a very critical review of it.
Wright responded vigorously and a literary debate was initiated between the two. One of the New York academies saw this as an opportunity, and invited Wright and Mumford to continue their debate
in public. Both accepted.*

*They appeared before a very large audience at the appointed time and
place. In deference to his seniority, Wright was given the opportunity
to open the debate. He rose, turned to Mumford and asked, "Mr.
Mumford, have you ever designed a building?"*

Mumford replied, "No."

*"Then," asked Mr. Wright, "what right do you have to criticize anyone
who has?"*

*Mumford replied, "Mr. Wright, I have never laid an egg, but I can
sure tell the difference between a good one and a bad one."*

MORAL: Even a good egg can lay a bad one.

Mumford's response was deceptively clever. It was not until
much later that I grasped its irrelevance: it wasn't possible for
Mr. Mumford to tell a chicken how to lay a better egg; it was
possible for him to tell an architect how to design a better
building. It was not the validity of Mumford's criticism that
Wright was challenging, but the fact that it could not be used
constructively.

In most of the several hundred organizations in which I have
conducted research or planning, I have had no prior knowledge
of the service or product around which the organization was
organized. Yet, without such knowledge it would have been
impossible to help these organizations. The old man on the
railroad's board was right: one does have to know something
about railroads to help them. However, the fact that I didn't

have such knowledge did not prevent my helping the railroad, because I did not have to do so alone. By participating on a team that included someone who had this knowledge, I could help the railroad, and I did.

In fact, my lack of an intimate knowledge of railroading turned out to be a great advantage to the team. It enabled me to look at the railroad in new and different ways. I could ask many more irreverent but relevant questions than those who knew the system well. To know a system well is to know how it operates, but not necessarily why it operates the way it does.

Transition

Recall my previous assertions that ". . . development is more a matter of learning than of earning, and learning is obviously a matter of education. What is not so obvious is that education is not necessarily a matter of schooling. One can get an education without going to school, and one can go to school without getting an education."

The reason for all this is that our educational system focuses on teaching rather than learning. It does so with the mistaken notion that teaching is an effective way of producing learning. This is a mistake which I explore in the next chapter.

Chapter Three

Never Let Your Schooling Interfere with Your Education

Becoming an Antibureaucrat

❦ ❦ ❦

Every child is an artist. The problem is how to
remain an artist when he grows up.

—Picasso

❦ ❦ ❦   *Adherence to Type*

One year, after many of struggling with students' handwriting on term papers, I issued a set of specifications as to how I wanted their papers presented. They were to be typed, double spaced, on 8½-by-11-inch white paper, unlined, with approximately a one-inch margin on all sides.

When I distributed these instructions at the beginning of the semester, I asked if there were any questions. There were several, which I answered. They did not require modification of my specifications.

Among the papers I received at the end of the semester was one that was typed across the long dimension of the paper rather than the short one, as is the usual practice. At the end of this paper the author wrote, "Aha. I gotcha."

My initial reaction was anger, because it was apparent that the student knew perfectly well what I wanted. However, on reflection I realized that he took my specifications as a challenge. What he had done was creative, and this was more important than the content of his paper, which was not bad. I gave him an A, but admonished him that the next time he did it it would no longer be creative.

> **MORAL: Teachers kill creativity by inducing students to give them the answers that students think teachers expect. Answers that are expected cannot be creative.**

Industrialized Schooling

Most of our schools, including colleges and universities, are industrialized disseminators of information. They are modeled after factories. Incoming students are treated like raw material that is put on a production line for conversion into a finished product. Each step in the process is prescribed and scheduled. The processed material is inspected and tested periodically. If its quality falls below a specified minimum, it is rejected by the system. If the number of rejects gets too large, the requirement for acceptance is more likely to be reduced than the process is to be modified. The output of each educational production run is intended to be of uniform quality. The finished product is branded and given a model number (for example, "Harvard '89"). The process is considered successful if its products can be sold at a high price and if their purchasers subsequently feel they have received good value for their money.

Industrialized education treats students like things that are expected to have the combined properties of tape recorders, cameras, and computers: that is, to be able to reproduce exactly whatever has been presented to them. Most examinations are tests of this reproductive ability.

Those at the leading edge of industrialized education have even mechanized the production line (the teacher) with computer-assisted instruction (CAI) and programmed learning. They program computers to try to make students remember as much and as accurately as the computers do. If industrially oriented educators knew how to program students directly, they would undoubtedly do so.

What Students Need to Know

The preoccupation of educators with what students need to know can only be justified if the educators know (1) what the students are going to do after their graduation, and (2) what they are going to need to know to do it well. Educators know neither.

Within a short time after graduation many, if not most, graduates practice in a field other than the one in which they were educated. In a report prepared for the Carnegie Foundation, W.G. Ireson noted:

> The most important fact brought out by . . . surveys over a period of 30 years is that more than 60 percent of those persons who earned [engineering] degrees in the United States either became managers of some kind within 10 to 15 years or left the engineering profession entirely to enter various kinds of business ventures. . . .[1]

In an editorial in *Science*, Dael Wolfle[2] wrote that one-fifth of Americans awarded doctorates move out of the field in which they received their degrees within five years after receiving them, and 35 percent do so within 15 years.

Not one member of the faculty in the department of The Wharton School from which I recently retired had ever taken a course, let alone a degree, in a business school.

The accelerating rate of change, particularly technological, rapidly obsoletes much of what we know. It reduces the effectiveness of experience as a teacher. The fact that one has driven an automobile for 25 years does not equip one to pilot a jet airplane or a spacecraft. It has been estimated that about 50 percent of what is currently relevant in most professions will not be relevant within five years. Such transience of knowledge is reflected in the story of the ex-student who, a decade after graduation, visited his old professor of economics. When the ex-student entered the professor's office he was grading examinations. The ex-student picked one up and looked through it. Then he remarked to the professor, "This is the same set of questions you gave us 10 years ago." "Yes," said the professor, "but the answers have changed."

There appear to be a few subjects that we can be relatively sure students will need. Traditionally, we have taken these to be reading, writing, and arithmetic. However, arithmetic is no longer necessary; a hand calculator is faster, more accurate, and can carry out more mathematical operations than most brains. Furthermore, we already have machines that can read print aloud and can convert voice to print. They may eventually replace the need to read and write, at least in part.

My point is not that it will not be advantageous to be able to read, write, and calculate, but that these abilities may well not be needed. In the future, there may not be any subject that must be known for a useful adulthood other than how to use the machines that know the subjects needed.

From Data to Wisdom

An ounce of information is worth a pound of data.

An ounce of knowledge is worth a pound of information.

An ounce of understanding is worth a pound of knowledge.

Despite this, most of the time spent in school is devoted to the transmission of information and ways of obtaining it. Less time is devoted to the transmission of knowledge and ways of obtaining it (*analytic thinking*). Virtually no time is spent in transmitting understanding or ways of obtaining it (*synthetic thinking*). Furthermore, the distinctions between data, information, and so on up to wisdom are seldom made in the educational process, leaving students unaware of their ignorance. They not only don't know, they don't know what they don't know.

The reason so little understanding is transmitted by teachers is that they have so little to transmit. They are more likely to know *what* is right than *why* it is right. Most why questions do not have unique and simple answers, and therefore are difficult to use in examinations or to grade when they are used. Explanations require discussion if they are to produce understanding. The ability to lead fruitful discussions is not an attribute of most teachers. Therefore, to break this educational logjam we have to develop ways by which students can gain understanding without having it taught to them. The fact is that most of the understanding that most of us acquire we acquire on our own, without it having been taught to us. Thus, what is required of the educational system is release of this ability to gain understanding on our own and encouragement to use it. Such a release may even enable teachers to gain some understanding.

Data are symbols that represent the properties of objects and events. Information consists of processed data, the processing directed at increasing its usefulness. For example, census takers collect data. The Bureau of the Census processes that data, converting it into information that is presented in the numerous tables published in the *Statistical Abstracts*. Like data, information also represents the properties of objects and events, but it does so more compactly and usefully than data. The difference between data and information is functional, not structural.

Information is contained in *descriptions*, answers to questions that begin with such words as who, what, when, where, and how many. *Knowledge* is conveyed by instructions, answers to how-to questions. *Understanding* is conveyed by explanations, answers to why questions.

Information, knowledge, and understanding enable us to increase efficiency, not effectiveness. The efficiency of behavior or an act is measured relative to an objective by determining either the amount of resources required to obtain that objective with a specified probability, or the probability of obtaining that objective with a specified amount of resources. The value of the objective(s) pursued is not relevant in determining efficiency, but it is relevant in determining effectiveness. *Effectiveness is evaluated efficiency.* It is efficiency multiplied by value, efficiency for a valued outcome.

Intelligence is the ability to increase efficiency; wisdom is the ability to increase effectiveness.

The difference between efficiency and effectiveness—that which differentiates wisdom from understanding, knowledge, information, and data—is reflected in the difference between development and growth. Growth does not require an increase in value; development does. Therefore, development requires an increase in wisdom as well as understanding, knowledge, and information.

Wisdom deals with values. It involves the exercise of judgment. Evaluations of efficiency are all based on a logic that, in principle, can be programmed into a computer and automated. These evaluative principles are impersonal. We can speak of the efficiency of an act independently of the actor. Not so for effectiveness. A judgment of the value of an act is never independent of the judge, and seldom is the same for two judges.

From all this I infer that although we are able to develop computerized information-, knowledge-, and understanding-generating systems, we will never be able to generate wisdom by such systems. It may well be that wisdom—which is essential for the pursuit of ideals or ultimately valued ends—is the characteristic that differentiates man from machines. For this reason, if no other, the educational process should allocate as much time to the development and exercise of wisdom as it does to the development and exercise of intelligence.

Not only does schooling do little or nothing about the generation of understanding and the development of wisdom, it does little about even the collection of data and the generation of information. There are great subtleties involved in the collection of data and its conversion into information. Most of these subtleties are not revealed in the educational process. Most of us have to learn them the hard way.

❦ ❦ ❦   *On Foaming at the Mouth*

When Busch beer was being introduced to the market, I was asked to determine how beer drinkers compared its taste with competitive products. My colleagues and I designed what we thought was a good procedure for conducting the taste tests required. We took Busch and three other beers, removed all identification from their bottles, and then labeled the beers using letters—A, B, C, D, and E. We formed two groups of Busch beer using different letters for each group. We wanted to determine how reliable were the comparisons made by our subjects.

Only regular drinkers of one of the four brands of beer used in the test were subjects. They were invited to beer-tasting evenings at prominent hotels in the centers of the cities in which the tests were conducted. Each subject was given five bottles of beer and asked to rank them by taste. They were free to conduct their trials as they saw fit.

The average ranking of each beer was then determined. Much to our surprise, the difference in the average rankings of the two differently labeled groups of Busch beer was very different. This made no sense and, of course, cast considerable doubt on the reliability of the results.

I lamented over this to August A. Busch III, now CEO of Anheuser-Busch companies but then a junior vice president in charge of the Busch brand. He expressed no surprise at the results. He asked me how people actually make their choices between competing brands. Do they line up bottles of the competing brands and sip-test them, as we had them do in our test? Of course not. Then why didn't we have them test the brands as they would normally?

We went back to the drawing board and redesigned the test. This time we placed cases of unmarked bottles of the competing beers in the homes of regular beer drinkers and gave them a month to compare the brands in any way they wanted. At the end of a month we collected their rankings. The results were completely different from those we had obtained in the first test, and they corresponded to the ranking of the market shares of the beers tested. In addition, the rankings of the two cases of differently lettered Busch beer were essentially the same.

> **MORAL: The right information cannot be extracted from the wrong data.**

In retrospect, the reason for the failure of the first beer taste test and the success of the second was obvious. As a pipe smoker, for example, I often tried a pipeful of tobacco I had never tried before. I frequently enjoyed that first pipeful enough to buy a package of that tobacco. In most cases I was unable to finish it. Preferences over the long haul can be quite different from those over the short haul. The staying power of a product is at least as important as the initial impression it makes.

Poor teaching of inferential statistics has led to major errors in processing data into information. Students are taught to perform numerous statistical operations without understanding them at all. As a result, they extract misinformation from data and cannot tell the difference between the information and misinformation produced by others. Among the more common types of error frequently committed are the following:

First, statistics provide a way of arriving at inferences from a sample drawn in a prescribed way from a well-specified population to that population. Inferences arrived at from samples drawn in other ways are not valid. Nevertheless, they are commonly made. For example, one research team studied the characteristics of 30 ulcer patients in a particular hospital to which they had access. They drew inferences from their study of this group of patients to ulcer patients in general. Such inferences are completely unjustified. What they had was not a random sample drawn from the large population of interest to them, but a smaller population of interest. Treating it as a random sample is illegitimate, so are inferences drawn from one population to another.

Second, correlation analysis is one of the most frequently used ways of processing data. It provides a measure of the association between variables, the degree to which they tend to change in the same or opposite directions. For example, height and weight of people are correlated positively because they tend to increase/decrease together. Unfortunately, those who find a correlation between variables often erroneously infer that one of them *causes* the changes in the other. This is as wrong as inferring from their correlation that an increase in weight will produce an increase in height. The conclusion drawn from correlation—as was done frequently in studies of the relationship between cigarette smoking and lung cancer—may be right, but the inferential process by which it was obtained is wrong.

Third, in estimating the value of a variable, two types of error can be made: overestimation and underestimation. (Corresponding types of error are involved in the other major activity of inferential statistics: testing hypotheses.) Either of these types of error can be reduced by changing statistical estimating procedures. However, whenever the probability of one of these types of error is decreased, the probability of the other is increased. To determine which combination of these types of error is more desirable requires knowledge of the costs associated with each. Few of those who use statistics to make estimates know the costs of error or are even aware of their relevance. They use conventional estimating procedures, almost all of which assume costs of error that are much more likely to be wrong than right. For example, it is commonly assumed that the cost of an overestimate of a specified magnitude is equal to the cost of an underestimate of the same magnitude. Can you imagine estimating the percentage of a chemical in a drug that is poisonous beyond a certain concentration and assuming that overestimating that percentage is just as costly as underestimating it by the same amount? The underestimate can result in death, but the overestimate may only reduce the potency of the drug.

When we speak of the lack of understanding produced by school, we should include lack of understanding of the methods by which we extract information, knowledge, and understanding from data.

The Medium versus the Message

Schools seems able to survive the serious trouble they are in with little if any change. This is not because little is done, but because what is done has little effect. What is done has little effect because the trouble schools are in is generally diagnosed incorrectly. Diagnostic efforts focus on what is taught, the content of teaching, the messages it delivers. However, much (if not most) of what students learn in the educational process is not derived from what is taught, but from how it is taught. In education, perhaps more than in any other domain, *the medium is the message*.

The principal characteristic of the educational process that affects what is learned and needs to be unlearned is its focus on what appears to be problem solving.

The Focus on So-Called Problems

The focus on problem solving is responsible for a great deal of the learning and unlearning students must engage in after they leave school. Throughout their formal education, students are evaluated by their ability to solve problems that are *given* to them. Therefore, it is only natural for them to go out into the world assuming that problems will continue to be given to them. However, nothing could be further from the truth. Outside of school, problems are seldom "given"; they usually have to be taken, extracted from complex situations. Students are not taught how to do this. They are not even made aware of the need to do it.

Problems, exercises, and questions. Most of what most teachers consider to be problems are not problems at all; they are exercises or questions, and most teachers, hence students, are unaware of the very important differences between them.

🐞 🐞 🐞   *Look Before You Speak*

I was once given the following problem by an eminent statistician: You dip into a bowl containing only black and white balls and pull out m *black balls and* n *white balls. Now, if you dip into the bowl again without replacing the balls you withdrew previously and pull out one ball, what is the probability that it will be white?*

I told him I would answer his question after he told me how he knew the bowl contained only white and black balls. "That," he said, "would ruin the problem." He didn't realize that he had already done so. Instead, he reformulated the problem.

This time, he said, the balls are all white on the outside and are contained in a clear bowl into which I could look. Some of the balls have black cores; the cores of the others are white. Now, he continued, if you dip into this bowl and pull out m *balls that, when split open, reveal black cores and* n *balls that reveal white cores, what is the probability that if you dip into the bowl again and withdrew one ball it would have a white core?*

"How," I asked, "do you know the balls have only white or black cores?"

He turned away in disgust and abandoned his effort to test me.

> **MORAL: An exercise is a problem from which at least some of the information required to formulate it is denied to the one asked to solve it.**

The very popular case method of teaching uses exercises, not problems. Much of the information used to formulate these exercises has been filtered out. To be sure, they contain what the author considers to be all the relevant information. But separation of the relevant information from the irrelevant is a critical part of problem formulation and solving, and what is relevant to one problem solver may not be to another. Nevertheless, some argue that what is learned in dealing with cases is useful in dealing with real problems. This is like arguing that learning how to box with one hand tied behind one's back is a good way to learn how to box with both hands.

A question is an exercise from which the reason for wanting to solve it has been removed. It is an unmotivated exercise, a problem with no context. *Nevertheless, the reasons for wanting to answer a question determines what is the right answer to it.* For example, even the question "How much is two plus two?" has no meaning out of context. The answer is not the same when the two refers to degrees Fahrenheit as it is when it applies to chairs.

To learn how to answer questions or solve exercises is not to learn how to solve problems; and to learn how to solve problems that are *given* is not to learn how to *take* problems from real situations, how to *formulate* them. For example, a recent study received national attention when it cited a growing shortage of university professors. It urged solution of this problem. However, it struck me that professors who are in class for no more than three to nine hours per week and who often give courses they have frequently given before are hardly being overworked, even if they are engaged in research. The formulation of the problem as a shortage of professors not only assumes that the amount of teaching they currently do is just right, it also assumes, among other things, that:

1. The number of courses required of students is just right, and fewer would be bad.

2. The number of contact hours between students and teachers is just right, and fewer would be bad.

3. The number of weeks per session is just right, and more would be bad.

4. The number of sessions per year is just right, and more would be bad.

Not one of these assumptions seems obviously true to me. What does seem obvious is that it would be easier and quicker to get rid of the shortage by manipulating the variables affected by the assumptions I have listed than by trying to produce more professors. Producing more professors might well perpetuate currently inefficient and ineffective practices.

A wrong solution to the right problem is generally better than the right solution to the wrong problem, because one usually gets feedback that enables one to correct wrong solutions, but not wrong problems. Wrong problems are perpetuated by right solutions to them.

Problem treatments. Students are seldom made aware of the fact that there are four different and unequally effective ways of dealing with problems: *absolution, resolution, solution,* and *dissolution.*

Absolution consists of ignoring a problem and hoping it will go away or solve itself.

Resolution consists of doing something that yields an outcome that is considered to be good enough, that "satisfices." (Clinicians tend to resolve problems. Resolutions rely heavily on past experience, trial and error, qualitative judgment, and common sense.)

Solution consists of doing something that yields what is currently considered to be the best possible outcome, one that optimizes. (This involves a research approach to problems, one that relies heavily on experimentation and quantitative analysis.)

Dissolution consists of redesigning the entity that has the problem or its environment so as to idealize: eliminate the problem and enable that entity to do better in the future than the best it can do now.

I have encountered only one problem situation in which all four approaches were made to the problem involved. Therefore, although I presented it in my last book, I repeat it here.

❦ ❦ ❦   *A Bus-y Problem*

A large city in Europe uses double-decker buses for public transportation. Each bus has a driver and a conductor. The driver is seated in a compartment separated from the passengers. The closer the driver keeps to schedule, the more he is paid. The conductor collects zoned fares from boarding passengers, issues receipts, collects these receipts from disembarking passengers, and checks to see that the correct fare has been paid. He also signals the driver when he need not stop to discharge passengers and when the bus is ready to move on after stopping to discharge or receive passengers. Undercover inspectors ride the buses periodically to determine whether the conductors collect all the fares and check all the receipts. The fewer misses they observe, the more the conductors are paid.

To avoid delays during rush hours, conductors usually let passengers board without collecting their fares because collecting fares immediately would extend the length of the stops. They try to collect the fares between stops. Because of crowded conditions on the bus, the conductor cannot always return to the entrance in time to signal the driver when there are no passengers to discharge or when, after stopping, he can move on. Unless the driver receives a signal not to stop, he must do so. If the driver receives no signal to move on, he must decide to do so himself by use of his side-view mirror. In either case, delays were caused that were costly to the driver and which he attributed to the conductor. As a result, hostility grew between drivers and conductors and eventually erupted in a number of violent episodes.

Management of the system first tried to ignore the problem, hoping that if it were left alone it would go away. This effort at absolution did not work; the number of violent incidents increased in number and intensity.

Management then tried to resolve the problem by proposing a return to an earlier state by eliminating incentive payments and accepting less-than-on-schedule performance. The drivers and the conductors rejected this proposal because it would have reduced their earnings.

Then management tried to solve the problem by having the drivers and conductors on each bus share equally the sum of the incentive payments due each. This proposal was also rejected by the drivers and conductors; they were opposed to cooperating in any way.

Finally, a problem dissolver was employed by management to deal with the situation. Instead of trying to compromise the conflicting interests of the drivers and conductors, he looked at the system as a whole. He found that during rush hours there were more buses in operation than there were stops in the system. Therefore, at his suggestion, conductors were moved off the buses at peak hours and placed at the stops. This reduced the number of conductors required at peak hours and made it possible to improve the distribution of their working hours. Under the new system, conductors collected fares during peak hours from people waiting for buses at the stops, and they were always at the rear entrance in position to signal drivers to move on. *Passengers were provided with a way to signal the driver when they wanted the bus to let them off. At off-peak hours, when the number of buses in operation was fewer than the number of stops, conductors returned to the buses.*

> **MORAL: Those who can't get on together can frequently do so when one of them gets off.**

Problems and disciplinarity. Schools beyond the elementary level are organized into disciplinary departments, and so are the courses and curricula they offer. The disciplines provide a convenient way of labeling and filing knowledge. But the world is not organized the way schools are. There are no physical, chemical, biological, psychological, sociological, or any type of disciplinary problems. Disciplinary adjectives before the word "problem" reveal absolutely nothing about the problem; what they reveal are the points of view of the persons looking at the problem.

❦ ❦ ❦   *Down on the Stairs Up*

A while ago some of my professorial colleagues and I were meeting with leaders of the self-development effort in the Philadelphia neighborhood previously referred to, Mantua. A member of the community broke into the meeting with bad news. That morning an 83-year-old woman who lived in the neighborhood and was very active in its development effort had gone to the area's only free health clinic for her monthly checkup. She had been told she was fine and left for home, a fourth-floor walkup. While climbing the third flight of stairs on the way to her rooms, she had a heart attack and died.

The silence that followed this announcement was eventually broken by the professor of community medicine, who said, "I told you we need more doctors at the clinic. If we had them, we'd be able to make house calls and this sort of thing wouldn't happen."

After another silence the professor of economics spoke up. "You know, there are plenty of doctors in Philadelphia who will make house calls. She just couldn't afford one. If her welfare or medical benefits had been adequate, she could have called one and this wouldn't have happened."

The professor of architecture then asked why elevators weren't required in all multiple-dwelling units of more than three floors.

Finally, the professor of social work spoke up. "You all seem to be unaware of the fact that she has a son who is a graduate of our university's law school. He is now a senior partner in a very prestigious law firm located in center city. He, his wife, and two children live in a very nice bungalow in an affluent suburb. If that woman and her son had not been alienated, she would have had no stairs to climb and all the money she needed to call a private practitioner."

MORAL: There are as many realities as there are minds contemplating them.

Learning how to determine what point(s) of view will produce the best treatment of a problem should be, but seldom is, an essential part of education.

Knowledge and understanding come as much from creative reorganization of what we already know as from the discovery of new things. Therefore, students should not be led to believe that current ways of classifying information, knowledge, and understanding involve fixed categories that are inherent in the nature of things. They should be encouraged to organize their learning in ways that best serve them, not the educational system. When we isolate and put boundaries around a subject, we inhibit exploration of its relationship by experts in other subjects. Disciplines are used to organize craft unions that are preoccupied with preserving their academic prerogatives. Academic departments and curricula do not organize knowledge; they organize teachers and *dis*organize knowledge.

It is important for students to realize that the best place to deal with a problem is not necessarily where the problem appears. For example, we don't try to treat headaches with brain surgery, but by swallowing a pill.

Problems are abstractions. Perhaps the most damaging problem-related misconception promulgated by the educational process is that problems are objects of direct experience. Problems are not experienced: they are abstractions extracted from experience by analysis. They are as related to what is experienced as atoms are related to tables. Tables are experienced, not atoms. What we experience are dynamic situations that consist of complex systems of problems, not individual or isolated problems. I call such systems *messes*.

A system is a whole whose essential properties are not to be found in any of its parts. For example, no part of an automobile can itself carry a person from one place to another. A human being, one of whose essential properties is the ability to write, has no part that can do so—not even his or her hand, which, when separated from the body, can do nothing. Therefore, the properties of a system derive from the *interactions* of its parts, not their actions taken separately. It follows that when a system is taken apart, it loses its essential properties. Furthermore, when a part of a system is separated from that system, it also loses its essential properties. For example, an automobile's motor cannot move even itself when separated from the automobile, and a hand separated from its arm can take hold of nothing.

Therefore, when a mess, which is a system of problems, is taken apart, it loses its essential properties and so does each of its parts. The behavior of a mess depends more on how the treatments of its parts interact than on how they act independently of each other. A partial solution to a whole system of problems is better than whole solutions to each of its parts taken separately. Nevertheless, students are taught to treat problem as separable, self-contained units. They are unaware of the existence or nature of messes and, of course, of ways of dealing with them.

By observing the way the educational system is organized and managed, students come to believe that a system's performance can be improved by improving the performance of each of its parts taken separately. Even in business schools, students do not learn that effective management of organized behavior is management of interactions, not actions. They are not even made aware of the differences between these types of management. What they are taught is that if they improve the performance of each part of a corporation taken separately, the performance of the corporation as a whole will be improved. This is absolutely false. Fortunately, improving the performance of each part taken separately does not necessarily make the whole perform as badly as possible. If it did, few corporations would survive as long as they do.

The quality of education provided by a school is not the sum of the qualities of the education provided by each of its departments, but the product of their interactions. Dealing with messes and organizations as a whole, with interactions rather than actions, requires synthetic, not analytic, thinking.

Analysis and Synthesis

The educational system equates analysis and thought, but analysis is only one way of thinking. It is a three-step process in which something to be understood is first taken apart or disaggregated. Then an effort is made to understand the behavior of each of its parts taken separately. Finally, understanding of the parts is aggregated in an effort to understand the whole.

Because analysis reduces a system to its parts, it loses the system's essential properties and, therefore, the ability to explain its behavior. It cannot yield understanding, only knowledge. For example, no amount of analysis of American and English automobiles can explain why their drivers sit on different sides of the automobile. Furthermore, because analysis also considers the parts of a system separately, it loses their essential properties and the ability to explain their behavior.

Explanation, the acquisition of understanding, requires synthetic thinking. Synthetic thinking, like analysis, involves three steps, but they are the inverse of those involved in analysis. In the first step of analysis the thing to be understood is taken apart; in synthesis it is taken to be a part of a larger whole. The larger containing whole(s) is/are identified. In the second step of analysis the behavior of each part is explained separately; in the second step of synthesis the behavior of the containing whole is explained. In the last step of analysis, the understanding of the parts is aggregated into an understanding of the whole; in synthesis, the understanding of the containing whole is disaggregated to explain the behavior or properties of that part which is to be explained. The behavior and properties of that part are explained by revealing its role or function in the larger whole of which it is part.

Analysis reveals the structure of a system, how it works. Its product is knowledge. Synthesis reveals why a system has the properties it has or works the way it does. Its product is understanding. Clearly we need, and need to know how to acquire, both knowledge and understanding. However, few students are even taught the difference between them, let alone the different thought processes by which they are obtained.

Teaching and Learning

Recall a portion of the earlier quotation from Illich: "The pupil is . . . 'schooled' to confuse teaching with learning . . ." The reason is that teachers confuse the two; they assume that teaching is an efficient producer of learning. One would think that this assumption would be seriously questioned by educators. After all, they are aware that we learned our first language well without having it taught to us, but seldom learn nearly as well a second language that is taught to us. We learn a great deal more from our experience than we do from those who are experienced.

❦ ❦ ❦   *Go and Stop Driving*

When my son, Alan, completed his first year at the California Institute of the Arts in Valencia, California, he returned to Philadelphia for the summer. He began almost immediately to work on me to buy an automobile for him. He reasoned that it would save him and me money when he went to or came from the West Coast, and he argued that a car was virtually essential for survival in California. I was not convinced, and refused. After a number of his unsuccessful efforts to change my mind, he became sufficiently desperate to look for a job. He found one working for a tree surgeon.

In the first week he fell out of a tree and hurt his leg enough to make it impossible for him to retain the job. Then he really went to work on me. He became a thorough and continuous pest. Finally, in an effort to make my own summer bearable, I told him I would lend him the money required to buy a car. This cheered him considerably. He went off enthusiastically in search of a car. Several days later he announced that he had found one. A friend of his was willing to sell him a 12-year-old Chevy for a very low price. I expressed the opinion that such a car was very unlikely to get him back to the West Coast, and was very likely to lead to his loss of a friend. My son assured me I was wrong on both counts. He told me he had taken the car to a third friend, who was a skilled auto mechanic, and he had checked the car over. It was fine.

Despite my advice to the contrary, my son bought that car and took off for the West Coast. The car broke down a number of times on the way, requiring repairs the cost of which exceeded the cost of the car. Eventually my son reached Las Vegas, where the car broke down and was no longer repairable. He disposed of it as scrap and hitchhiked the rest of the way back to his school. He also lost a friend.

When he returned home the following summer he wanted to know how I knew what would happen to him, the car, and his friendship. Because, I said, I had done essentially the same thing when I was his age. Then he wanted to know why I hadn't told him this. I asked him if he thought it would have made any difference. After a moment's reflection, he said, "No."

> **MORAL: One can learn a great deal from one's own mistakes, but practically nothing from those made by others.**

There are many things we insist on learning for ourselves. We resent having them taught to us. Observation of a child for a short time makes this apparent.

There are a variety of ways of learning without being taught. The effectiveness of each varies with time, the place, the subject matter, and the learner. Therefore, students should have maximum freedom to select those ways of learning that best suit them. Before considering ways of learning that are superior to being taught, consider some of the deficiencies of teaching.

What's Wrong with Teaching?

Four things are wrong with teaching. First, it is more concerned with transmitting than receiving. Second, it assumes ignorance on the part of students. Third, it discourages, if not kills, crea-

tivity. Fourth, it normally uses tests and examinations to determine what students have learned, and they do not do so
effectively. Consider each of these deficiencies in turn.

Transmitting versus receiving. We learn more by talking than
by listening, but most teachers do all or most of the talking,
imposing silence on their students most of the time. Talking
gives us an opportunity to discover—become aware of—what
we know and don't know. Children who are seen but not heard
do not learn very much. It would be much better educationally
if they were heard, even if not seen.

¥ ¥ ¥   *A Very Loud Silence*

*In my last year as a graduate student in philosophy at the University
of Pennsylvania, the philosophy department hired as an assistant professor a recent Ph.D. from Columbia University. While there, he had
studied under John Dewey, who was America's best known philosopher
at that time. Not surprisingly, the new assistant professor considered
himself an authority on Dewey.*

*In his first semester at Penn, this young professor offered a course in
contemporary philosophy focusing on Dewey's work. Several of the
precocious and arrogant graduate students who signed up for the
course, including me, also considered themselves to be experts on
Dewey. Therefore, in the first few sessions, the young professor never
got more than a few minutes into his prepared presentation before
questions began to be asked, throwing him off his course. In none of
these initial sessions was he able to complete his prepared presentation,
because the questions and their discussion did not let up until the end
of the class. The young professor was annoyed and thoroughly frustrated. He was able neither to demonstrate his expertise in the subject
matter of the course nor to differentiate himself from the students.
Therefore, he opened the fourth session of the seminar by announcing
that from then on there would be no questions or discussion until he
had completed his prepared presentation.*

When the professor finished his presentation that day and indicated that he was ready for questions and discussion, there was spontaneous silence in the room. After repeated but futile requests from the professor for discussion, he dismissed the class. The class had been a bore because it contained little the students did not already know.

The silent treatment, now deliberate, continued in the next two classes. Finally the frustrated young professor announced a return to the earlier format in which questions and discussion were permitted at any time. The class returned to normal. Learning and fun resumed.

> **MORAL: Silence is sometimes more eloquent than words.**

Although our talking to others is a good way to find out what *we* think about a subject, it is often a very poor way of learning what *they* think about it.

☙ ☙ ☙   **Back Talk**

A corporation's chief executive officer whom I know well initiated communication sessions between himself and all his employees. Once each year he visited each of his company's sites and gave a talk on the state of the company to all the employees located there. After his prepared remarks, he opened the floor for discussion and questions. There was usually plenty of both.

One year, shortly after completion of the executive's tour, a very damaging strike was called against his company by its unionized hourly-paid employees. The executive told me he could not understand their behavior. None of the issues over which the strike was called were raised at any of his communication sessions. "Why?" he asked.

I told him his meetings with the company's employees had been arranged for him to communicate to them, not for them to communicate to him. "Why not?" he asked. "They were free to raise any issues they wanted." I pointed out that in a meeting he calls and in which he makes a formal presentation, people tend to raise questions or issues *they think he expects or wants, particularly if they respect him, as they did. Would a parishioner publicly ask embarrassing questions of a minister after he had completed a sermon? One cannot hold an extended discussion of an important issue from a floor occupied by a large audience. I said that if he wanted to hear what his employees wanted to say he would have to ask them to arrange a meeting in which they made a presentation to him and he did the listening and subsequent questioning.*

He did just that and it worked.

MORAL: It is very difficult to listen while talking.

Assuming ignorance of students. Teachers frequently underestimate the amount their students already know. Such underestimation is not restricted to teachers in school. Many managers assume they know more about their subordinates' jobs than their subordinates do. This has become less and less true with increasing technological content of work and increasing education of workers. Nevertheless, few managers have learned to ask their subordinates for advice.

❦ ❦ ❦   *They Never Asked Me*

In the early 1980s I participated in the introduction of a quality-of-work-life program at Alcoa's Tennessee Operations. Managers at all levels were asked to establish boards consisting of themselves, their immediate superiors, and their immediate subordinates. These boards were empowered to do anything they could with the resources available to them that would improve the quality of work life of their members, provided that what they did did not prevent any other units from doing what they wanted. A procedure was set up to handle possible differences between units.

Very shortly after the boards were established, two participating unionized workers who took the rolls of sheet aluminum off the end of the mills that produced them did something that saved the Operations a very significant amount of money. The rolls of aluminum coming off the end of the mill were cylinders about five feet long, hollow in the middle. These were set on end near the end of the mill, where they remained until a forklift moved them to a storage area. The forklift was often delayed because of such things as an obstruction in the access aisle, mechanical failure of the truck, a run-down battery, and so on.

When the truck was delayed for a relatively long time, which happened frequently, the space in which the cylinders were temporarily stored filled up, leaving no room for others coming off the end of the mill. Then the two men unloading the mill would move some of the cylinders back by placing a foot against the bottom of the upright cylinder, pulling the top so as to tip it slightly, and rolling it to a new location farther from the end of the mill. Rolling the cylinder on the concrete floor crimped the edge of the sheet on the outside of the cylinder. This was a defect many purchasers would not accept. They returned many of these rolls. Reworking these rolls was very costly to the Operations.

Shortly after the quality-of-work-life program had been initiated, the two men who unloaded the mill acquired from the shipping room a number of sheets of very heavy quilted paper in which the rolls were wrapped when shipped. They laid several layers of this paper on the floor where the cylinders were normally stored temporarily. When they rolled cylinders over this softer surface, their edges were less damaged than previously. This saved the company a significant amount of money.

When I was told what these men had done, I went down to the shop floor to congratulate them. They were proud of their accomplishment and pleased with the congratulations. While chatting with them I asked how long they had known of the solution they had just implemented. Blushing, one of them mumbled, "About 15 years."

Surprised, I then asked the obvious question: "Why did you wait so long to implement it?" I will never forget their answer: "Because those sons of bitches never asked us before."

MORAL: The less we expect from others, the less we are likely to get from them.

What one learns depends not only on what questions one asks of others, but also on what questions they answer. In the Soviet Union I once encountered an outrageous refusal to answer a question.

❦ ❦ ❦   **The Guest of Horror**

In the 1970s I was one of the very few foreigners who attended an international conference held in the Azerbaijan Soviet Socialist Republic at Baku. We were herded into a corner and seated around an interpreter who whispered his simultaneous translations of the proceedings to us.

In one of the plenary sessions a senior and distinguished Russian scientist delivered a paper on the use of Game Theory in forecasting. It was not a good paper; his understanding of both Game Theory and forecasting left a lot to be desired.

After the paper had been delivered, the floor was opened for discussion. A young man rose and asked a very astute question that got right at the basic flaw in the presentation. Much to my surprise, the old man who delivered the paper ignored the question and called on another young man who had indicated that he, too, had a question. The second young man, obviously angered by the old man's failure to answer the first question, repeated that question.

The old man was furious, and blurted out, "When you have contributed to this field with such distinction as merits my attention, I will give it to you and your questions. Until then, I have no intention of doing so."

Now I was furious. I indicated that I had a question. As I was one of the guests of honor, the old man called on me immediately. I repeated the question asked by the two young men.

The old man was stunned and very angry. He began to mutter something, stopped, and left the auditorium with no further word. The session was immediately adjourned by its chairman.

> **MORAL:** *Learning begins with questions we cannot answer; it ends with questions we can.*

Creativity. Continuous progress toward the ideal of complete development requires creativity as well as wisdom, understanding, knowledge, information, and data. Although we have always placed a great deal of value on creativity, only recently have we begun to understand it.

Creativity is a process involving three steps:

1. *Identification of self-imposed constraints.* These consist of one or more fundamental assumptions that appear to us to be obviously true, on which our choice of behavior is based, and which significantly reduce the range of choices available to us.

2. *Denial of the validity of the assumption(s) identified.*

3. *Exploration of the consequences of such denial.*

The same three steps are involved in solving puzzles. A puzzle is a problem that we cannot solve because of a self-imposed constraint, an incorrect assumption that we make. Therefore, to solve a puzzle we must identify the constraining assumption, remove it, and explore the consequences of having done so. For example, consider the puzzle shown in Figure 1. It consists of a block of 16 cells containing 15 prisoners and a warden. The only way in or out of the block is through the warden's cell. Every cell in the block has a doorway connecting it to each of its adjacent cells.

The prisoner in the lower left-hand cell is unique. He is a homicidal maniac who must kill anyone he can reach, but, curiously, cannot tolerate the sight of a dead person. Should he see one, he passes out and remains unconscious for at least 24 hours.

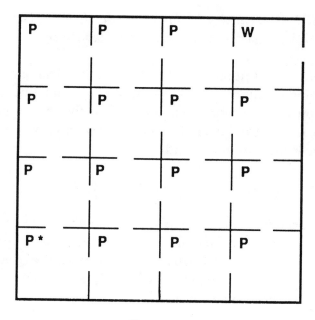

❦ *Figure 1*

One morning a visitor arrives at the block of cells and finds the warden and every prisoner except the maniac dead, each in his own cell. The maniac is gone. How did he get out?

As with most puzzles, one has to try the obvious first to see exactly what the problem is. It becomes apparent when we try what appears to be the most direct route out of the block of cells (Figure 2). The maniac cannot walk back through the last four cells he went through because they contain dead people, but he would have to go through them to escape.

In this case the principal self-imposed constraint that prevents solution of the puzzle is the assumption that the maniac cannot go back through *any* cell. He can return to one cell: his own. Once this is realized, a solution is easily found (Figure 3).

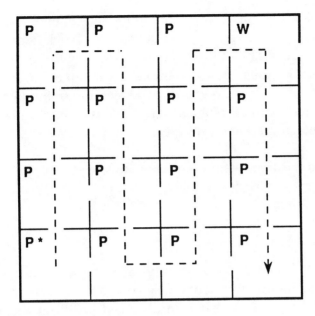

☙ *Figure 2*

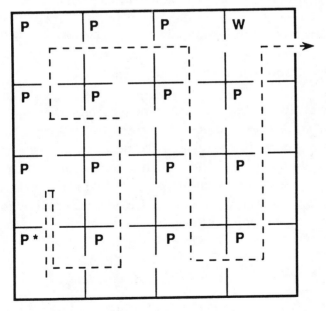

☙ *Figure 3*

Creativity is required for continuous development. Although improvement is possible without creativity, such improvement tends to be slight—for example, in automobiles from year to year. Breakthroughs—for example, invention of the airplane—require creativity. Creativity produces discontinuities, large qualitative changes. Not all such changes are efficient or effective, but progress requires creative outputs that are.

As with wisdom, we do not know how to teach creativity, but we do know how to stimulate and enhance it.[3] We also know how to kill it.

Tests and Examinations

The tests used by many educational institutions to determine the suitability of applicants have come under such an intense barrage of criticism that I hardly need dwell on them here. Suffice it to say that whatever it is they measure, it is not the ability to learn. At most, it is what has been learned; at worst, what has been memorized. There is no pressure on the authors of these examinations to make them measure what institutions want, because the institutions have come to want what these tests measure without knowing what this is.

How much students learn depends on more than the ability to learn; it also depends on opportunities to learn. The lack of such opportunities is responsible for the poor performance of many students, even those with a great ability to learn. High scores on tests are evidence of an ability to take tests, not necessarily of an ability to learn. Tests should provide an opportunity for learning, but seldom do. In many cases they don't even measure what has been learned.

❦ ❦ ❦   *On Reassembling a Broken Language*

In order to receive my doctorate in philosophy I had to demonstrate proficiency in two languages, one primary and the other secondary. I chose French as my primary language and German as the secondary. Both examinations consisted of a written translation of a passage from an undesignated book, without the use of a dictionary in the primary-language examination, and with a dictionary in the other.

The prospect of the French examination was not worrisome; I had studied French for three years in high school and four years in college. However, because it had been about five years since my last course, I needed to familiarize myself with that language. To this end I withdrew from the philosophy section of the university's library the first book in French I saw. It happened to be a book by Renan, L'Avenir de Science (The Future of Science). I dipped into this book periodically over the summer, using a dictionary to reinforce and expand my French vocabulary.

German was another matter. I had never studied this language. At a friend's suggestion I bought a little book called Minimum German and went to work trying to learn the elements of that language. The effort was excruciating. After a few weeks I gave up and placed the little hope I had of passing the German examination on my ability to use a dictionary. Then an unexpected and seemingly very fortunate thing happened: a classmate who had been raised by German-born parents and who was himself fluent in the language offered to tutor me. He had to take the same examination as I, but German was no problem for him.

He began to tutor me, but before long neither of us could stand the pain. I found the memorization required to learn the language abhorrent, and he found my ineptness discouraging. For the sake of our friendship, we gave up.

Fall came and with it the two examinations. The one in French came first. Incredibly, it consisted of a passage from Renan's book, a passage I remembered having translated that summer. I passed this one easily.

The French connection did not reduce my apprehensiveness about the German examination. My friend and ex-tutor was full of confidence. We went into the examination together. The passage we were asked *to translate was taken from Hegel's* Philosophy of Right. *The passage was very difficult. It has been wisely said of Hegel that his work cannot be translated into German, let alone any other language.*

I went to work on the assigned passage, furiously using a dictionary. I finished translating the passage about a half hour short of the three hours we had available. When I read what I had written, it made absolutely no sense. I was convinced there was no way my translation could be accepted. In desperation, I got a fresh examination book (in which we wrote our translations) and, using what I knew of Hegel but not of German, I wrote in English what I thought Hegel had said in the passage we were given.

Lo and behold, I passed the examination! However, my friend and ex-tutor, who translated the passage from Hegel literally, didn't. I think he still blames me for this.

MORAL: Examinations are not so much a matter of revealing how much one knows as of concealing what one does not know.

Closed-book examinations—the type most frequently used—are poor tests of knowledge and understanding because they are not like any real-life situations in which a person's knowledge and understanding are tested and evaluated. In real life people are evaluated by how well they get jobs done. They are expected to use all the resources available to them. In closed-book examinations students are expected to use none of the resources available to them. What students need to learn is what resources are available and how to use them effectively.

If examinations are used to evaluate students—and I don't believe they need be—they should be modeled on evaluative processes used in the real world. Open-book, take-home, and oral examinations are closer to such processes than closed-book examinations. Furthermore, an examination in which students prepare all or some of the questions as well as the answers reveals much more of their grasp of subjects than do conventional examinations. It enables them to identify those parts of a subject that they consider to be important and to explain why. In general, examinations reveal more about the examiner than the examinee.

None of us requires examinations to evaluate those with whom we work closely. Similarly, faculty members who work closely with students on common projects do not need examinations to determine what their students know. A teacher who does not know his students in this way is working them, but not working with them.

Alternatives to Teaching

1. Some subjects are best learned by teaching them to others. This is common knowledge among those who have taught. When teachers present subject matter that is new to them, they invariably learn it better than do any of their students. Therefore, many subjects, particularly those that are well organized and recorded in books, can be learned better by teaching them to others than by being taught by others. This is apparent when we reflect on the fact that teachers are educated more by their teaching than by what they were taught.

Small groups of three to eight students can be organized into *learning cells* in which each one teaches the others different subjects or different parts of the same subject. Cells can also be formed in which students teach faculty members subjects they do not know but students think they ought to. I recall with great satisfaction a cell devoted to national planning in less-developed countries given by a group of students to five faculty members. The student who organized that course was Francisco R. Sagasti, now a senior strategic planner at the World Bank.

Those acting as the teachers can help learning cells in several ways. First, they can specify the material they believe should be learned and the principal sources that can be used in doing so. Second, they can serve as resources to be used by the students as the students choose.

Students who have already learned a subject, by whatever means, can teach it to students at a lower level. This enables students who know a subject to consolidate and internalize their learning. It is already commonplace in universities to use graduate students to instruct undergraduates. This practice can be extended to all levels in the schooling process. It was used successfully at the Oak Lane Day School outside of Philadelphia by an elementary grade teacher, Mary Rees.

Teaching a computer can be a much more effective way of learning than being taught by a computer.

❦ ❦ ❦   *Computer-Obstructed Instruction*

A number of years ago, when computer-assisted instruction (CAI) was in its infancy, I was taken on a tour of the R&D facilities of a major computer manufacturer. I was told by the executive who was my guide that the company had recently supported development of a CAI program that had been installed in a West Coast elementary school. The program, I was told, had been developed by a professor whom I recognized as one of the best-known proponents of CAI. My escort told me he had a film that showed the program in operation.

I was shown a film of youngsters seven to eight years old being taught arithmetic by computers. They were seated at terminals, thoroughly engrossed, obviously excited, and having a good time. A teacher roamed around the room, occasionally stopping to make a comment or instruct a student. Students and teachers expressed enthusiasm for the program when they were interviewed in the film.

When the showing of the film was completed I was asked if I had any questions. I did. "How far into the course was the film made—early, middle, or at its end?" My escort and the others present did not know and they did not see the relevance of my question. I asked them to indulge me and find out. They phoned the author of the program and asked. The film had been made early in the course.

Then I asked what had happened to the children by the end of the course. Again they did not know. This time I suggested they call the school in which the program had been run and ask. Again they failed to see the relevance of my questions and again I asked them to indulge me.

They called the school and learned that most of the children had been withdrawn from the course by their parents because of the children's complaints about their boredom. They were "tired of the computers"; the novelty had worn off.

I did not have to explain why I had asked my questions.

MORAL: All's well that ends well, not begins well.

In the early 1950s, Stuart Cooke, then a professor at Case Institute of Technology, taught second grade students at the Hawkins School how to use a large computer to do their arithmetic homework. The students taught the computer what we wanted the students to learn. They had to do arithmetic well in order to get the computer to do their exercises correctly, and they had fun doing it. Mastering a complicated machine gave them an increased sense of their own importance. It was a humanizing, rather than a dehumanizing, experience.

If computerized education is to become effective it will have to facilitate students working together in social situations—learning from, teaching, and examining each other. Again back in the 1950s, some of my colleagues and I, together with experts

❦ *Figure 4*

in the educational division of Philco-Ford, developed the following computer-based learning system:

Three consoles with cathode-ray tubes, typewriters, and light-
pen inputs were arranged in a triangle (Figure 4) so that each
of three students could see and talk with the other two. None,
however, could see the screens facing the others. The computer
addressed the same question to each of the students in writing
on their screens. They answered either by use of a light pen or
keyboard. If fewer than all the answers were correct, the computer informed them of this, but nothing more. Then the
students—through discussion, reading, consultation with others, and any other means they wanted—had to try to discover
who had been right. When they agreed on the answer to be
given, they returned to the computer and tried again. The com-

puter would not proceed to the next question until all the answers submitted to it were correct. The students taught each other; the computer did no teaching, but it did facilitate learning.

Most teachers, particularly those at higher levels, have demonstrated an ability to learn effectively. For example, I was once asked by a student when I had last given a course on a subject that had existed when I was a student. The answer was 1951. This meant that everything I have taught since then was something I had to learn not by being taught, but on my own or by teaching. Teachers generally know much more about how to learn than about teaching.

2. Some subjects are best learned by teaching them to oneself. This is particularly true for subjects that one is highly motivated to learn. Such learning may involve using others as resources, but in a way that the learner, not the teacher, sees fit. The option of learning a subject on one's own—independent study—should be open to every student at any time.

❦ ❦ ❦   *What a Student Drug In*

Shortly after a number of my colleagues and I had completed what we considered a successful study directed at finding out why people consume alcoholic beverages, a graduate student, Robert Cort, approached me with a suggestion. He said he thought our findings could, with modification, be used to determine why people used addictive drugs. He admitted he knew nothing about such drugs or their usage, but that he would like time to look into the relevant literature and see if his hunch was worth pursuing. He asked for and received financial aid that enabled him to go his own way for about three months.

During that time he buried himself in the relevant literature and absorbed a large part of it. Then he prepared a proposal for research into the causes of addictive-drug usage. I was sufficiently impressed by his proposal to submit it to the National Institute of Health. We were awarded a grant of several hundred thousand dollars to conduct the study.

Bob Cort was subsequently asked to lecture on drug addiction at the medical school of the University of Pennsylvania.

> **MORAL: Curiosity may kill cats, but it seldom hurts students.**

At a meeting of the American Statistical Association called to celebrate one of its anniversaries, four distinguished contributors to the discipline were invited to speak. It turned out that not one of them had ever had a course in statistics. It is not at all uncommon that major contributions to the development of a field of study are made by people who have had no formal education in it.

The principal objective of education should be to enable students to learn how to learn and to motivate them to do so continuously. Despite this, faculties agonize over courses they believe students should take. But their objective is not student learning—it is faculty teaching.

3. Some skills are best learned through demonstration and instruction by one who already has that skill. For example, sports, surveying, drafting, fine arts, and use of laboratory equipment are best learned in this way. No amount of lecturing can by itself teach one how to ride a bicycle. Although one can learn these things on one's own, learning with the help of a good instructor is more rapid and effective.

4. Awareness of questions that have not been asked or answered is best acquired in seminars guided by one steeped in the relevant subject matter. Such seminars can also provide syntheses of what has already been learned.

At least as much education should be devoted to learning how to raise questions as to learning how to answer them. The American anthropologist Jules Henry once wrote:

> If all through school the young were provoked to question the Ten Commandments, the sanctity of revealed religion, the foundations of patriotism, the profit motive, the two-party system, monogamy, the laws of incest, and so on, we would have more creativity than we could handle.[4]

Ronald Laing, a prominent British psychiatrist, reacted to this:

> What schools do is to induce children to want to think the way school wants them to think. "What we see," in the American kindergarten and early schooling process, says Henry, "is the pathetic surrender of babies." You will, later or sooner, in the schools or in the home. It is the most difficult thing in the world to recognize this in our own culture.[5]

Education should also be concerned with a continuing synthesis of what is being learned and with an explicit formulation of a *weltanschauung*, a world view. Such a view makes it possible to convert data into information, information into knowledge, knowledge into understanding, and understanding into wisdom. These conversions are necessary for continuous personal development.

5. Many students are best motivated to learn and best learn how to learn by attempting to solve real problems under real conditions with guidance from one who already knows how — that is, by apprenticeship or internship. Apprenticeship and internship are effective ways of learning (1) how to make effective use of what one knows, (2) what one does not know but ought to know, and (3) how to learn it. They also motivate learning. Therefore, students should work on research or service projects directed at problems in the real world with faculty members or others who have relevant knowledge and experience. These projects should be carried out with the participation of those who have responsibility for doing something about them.

Such practice may have to take place out of school. R.C. Quittenton, president of St. Clair College of Applied Arts and Technology in Windsor, Ontario, saw this. He recommended

> that increased emphasis be put on work-study projects and out-of-classroom learning experiences. . . . We may eventually have no classroom lectures or formal labs and shops at all. Furthermore, some students . . . may never be on campus, because that is not where the action is. . . .[6]

These conditions are already being met by the Union Institute of Cincinnati, whose programs are attached to widely dispersed faculty members who are primarily engaged in practicing their arts and sciences.

6. Finally, traditional teaching and lecturing should be available to those who want them, but with as wide a choice of teachers as is possible. Not all faculty members can lecture well. A good lecturer on videotape is better than a poor one in person. Exciting lectures, seminars, and even tutorials should be recorded so that other students can see and hear them at their convenience. In time, any student in any school should have access to any faculty member in any school by means of such recordings. Videotapes could keep alive those outstanding stimulators of learning who have retired or died.

An Alternative to Teachers

About a decade ago, Fernando Solana, then secretary of education in Mexico, wanted to bring education to the large number of rural communities in his country. There were not enough qualified teachers to supply these communities. Solana engaged recent graduates from nearby high schools, promising them a college education if they would spend a few years in rural teaching. Subsequent tests given to students taught by these high school graduates and to students taught by professionals in Mexico City's schools revealed no significant difference in their educational attainment.

Conclusion

The deficiencies in the educational system cannot be removed by changing only the content of education. It requires fundamental redesign of the educational system and the processes in which it engages. The messages its structure and processes deliver are more seriously misleading and counterproductive than any messages delivered in courses.

What serves education well at any one time and place may not do so at another, or for different students. Therefore, we must give up the search for one best educational system, one that operates optimally regardless of time, place, and students. What is required is a system that can learn in, and adapt to, the conditions under which it must operate.

Summarizing, the educational system should

1. preserve individual differences among students, and encourage students to develop their unique combinations of competencies, not mold themselves into standardized, branded products.

2. focus on learning, not teaching, enabling students to learn how best to learn and motivating them to want to learn continuously.

3. synthesize what students learn so as to produce understanding if not wisdom (not merely transmit information and knowledge), and emphasize the interrelationships between subjects and disciplines, particularly between science, technology, and the arts and humanities.

4. enable students to deal with systems as a whole rather than reducing them by analysis to more easily treated parts.

5. encourage the continuous redesign of educational institutions and processes so they can be debureaucratized, demonopolized, and adapted to changing conditions and students, allowing students, their parents, and other stakeholders to participate in such redesign and in planning its implementation.

Chapter Four

A Great Many People Think They Are Thinking When They Are Merely Rearranging Their Prejudices

The Costs of Discrimination

❦ ❦ ❦

Fairness, justice, or whatever you call it—it's
essential and most companies don't have it.
Everybody must be judged on his performance, not
on his looks or his manners or his personality or
who he knows or is related to.

—Robert Townsend, *Up the Organization*

☙ ☙ ☙   *Son of a Bitch*

Herman Wrice is a black leader of Mantua, a so-called urban black ghetto located just north of the University of Pennsylvania in Philadelphia. He and I have been associated in his neighborhood's self-development efforts for more than two decades. This association has been a source of continuous learning for me. What I have learned most from Herman is a different way of looking at things. He has given me a glimpse of the black point of view, and I have acquired some understanding of the advantages of that perspective.

In a meeting Herman and I once attended, Herman was asked, "How will you know when you've reached your ultimate objective?"

Herman's reply was instantaneous: "When I'm able to call a black man a son of a bitch in front of white people like you and not feel guilty."

MORAL: To be discriminated against is to be cursed by those who do the discriminating, and to be inhibited from cursing the others who are discriminated against.

Herman's view of equality had never occurred to me. To me, if not most of us, equality means equality of opportunity. All other types of equality are subsumed under this general concept. However, this concept does not appear to include not feeling guilty about the use of profanity or obscenity when addressing someone of one's own or another race before a multiracial public. This can only be done when there is no discrimination, no distinction between *us* and *them*.

On the other hand, although white drivers of automobiles often make profane remarks to offensive white drivers of other automobiles, they seldom make such remarks to equally offensive black drivers. When asked why, they say that doing so could be interpreted as racial prejudice. Some will admit that fear of a violent reaction is also a deterrent. *We* almost always attribute to *them* a tendency to react violently. Whatever the reasons for whites holding back their reaction to offensive black drivers, doing so is a perverse type of discrimination.

The Nature of Discrimination

To discriminate is to distinguish between them and us and to treat them less well than us. This type of distinction is probably the most destructive we make in our lifetimes. Ronald Laing, the eminent British psychiatrist, put it this way:

> The brotherhood of man is evoked by particular men according to their circumstances. But it seldom extends to all men. In the name of freedom and our brotherhood we are prepared to blow up the other half of mankind, and to be blown up in turn.
>
> The matter is of life-and-death importance in the most urgent possible sense, since it is on the basis of such primitive social fantasies of who and what are I and you, he and she, We and They, that the world is linked or separated, that we die, kill, devour, tear and are torn apart, descend to hell or ascend to heaven, in short, that we conduct our lives.[1]

We think of ourselves either as superior to, or threatened by, *them*. We view *them* as either inferiors or enemies. The belief in our superiority is used to rationalize the preferential treatment we expect from *them* and other members of *us*. We try to keep *them* in their place. "Keeping them in their place" is a euphemism for exploitation.

Discrimination often incorporates snobbery. A snob, according to *The American Heritage Dictionary* (1976), is "one who is convinced of and flaunts his social or other superiority." Even when we are the ones discriminated against, we are often convinced of our superiority, even if we do not flaunt it. The victims of discrimination generally invite more oppression when they flaunt their believed superiority.

When *they* are seen as an enemy, our objective is to defeat them, deprive them of the ability or opportunity to obtain those of their alleged objectives that we perceive as conflicting with ours.

Almost any personal characteristic provides a sufficient basis for discrimination, but experience shows that the "best" ones are those over which those discriminated against have no control, properties that were not a matter of choice—for example, race, religion of parents, nationality, age, and sex. Furthermore, the property employed in discrimination does not have to be real; it can be, and often is, imaginary, as the following incident shows.

☙ ☙ ☙   *Mistaken Identity*

When I was directing the operations research group at Case Institute of Technology, I proposed the appointment to our group of a recent graduate from a Midwestern university. I prepared and submitted the paperwork required and waited for the necessary approvals. The first

*administrator in the approval chain phoned and asked me to come and
see him about the proposed appointment.*

*After I arrived at his office and we had gone through the usual small
talk, he said he had reviewed my recommendation and thought the
young man involved was eminently qualified. However, he said, he
was concerned lest the appointment increase my group's "imbalance."
I knew him well enough to know that by imbalance he meant the
inclusion of too many Jews, but I pretended not to know what he
meant. I pressed him for clarification. This embarrassed him. He tried
hard to avoid stating his prejudice, but I persisted in my feigned
ignorance until, with great discomfort, he came out with it. However,
he assured me that he was not prejudiced; he was only concerned about
the unfavorable way potential corporate clients of our research services
might perceive those offering them.*

*I then told the administrator that, in fact, the young man involved
was not Jewish but had been born into a Greek Orthodox family, whom
I had met when I attended his wedding. I don't think I ever saw an
administrator as embarrassed as he was. He apologized profusely and
quickly brought our meeting to a close. I subsequently hired that young
man with no intervention from above.*

**MORAL: When a distinction that does not exist
makes a difference, it's more a matter of a distorted
mind than distorted vision.**

It is important to realize that when we differentiate *them* from
us, we define *us* as well as *them*. We are *them* to them, and *not-
them* to us. As Laing (1967) observed:

> The Them comes into view as a sort of social mirage. The Reds,
> the Whites, the Blacks, the Jews. In the human scene, however,
> such mirages can be self-actualizing. The invention of Them
> creates Us, and We may need to invent Them to reinvent Our-
> selves.[2]

Those who discriminate are often, but not always, a majority, and those discriminated against are often, but need not always be, a minority. Whites, a majority, discriminate against blacks, a minority; but the whites in South Africa, a minority, discriminate against the blacks, a majority. Women in the United States, a slight majority, are discriminated against by men, a slight minority. The Klu Klux Klan, a minority, discriminates against other minorities.

It is apparent that the victims of discrimination, whether a majority or minority, have less opportunity to develop than most of those who discriminate against them. In general, the targets of discrimination are given fewer and inferior opportunities for learning and have less access to socially provided resources. As a result, they usually experience a poorer quality of life and a lower standard of living than their discriminators.

What is not apparent is that the development of the discriminators is also obstructed by their acts of discrimination. The maintenance of discrimination is costly; it consumes resources and time that could otherwise be used either to develop or to realize more of the improvement of quality of life that development makes possible. This is reflected in an important study done by William Finnie[3] of the cost of discrimination against the blacks by whites in the United States.

When we discriminate against *them*, we remove *them* from the class of those from whom we believe we can learn anything useful. If nothing else, there is a great deal we can learn from those discriminated against about discrimination, segregation, prejudice, and their dehumanizing effects, as the fable that opened this chapter shows.

Responding to Discrimination

I wish I were capable of giving the kind of devastating retorts to infuriating discriminatory questions that Herman and my

other black friends give. As a youngster I read with great envy
the wonderful retorts published in *Reader's Digest*. Even today
I greatly admire the biting responses attributed to such wits as
Oscar Wilde and George Bernard Shaw. I feel the absence of
this skill most sharply when I witness a blatant act of discrimination. Unfortunately, almost all of the few perfect retorts I've
made were made after the fact, to myself.

✀ ✀ ✀   *Perfect Retorts*

*One of the best retorts to discrimination I have witnessed was made
by Forrest Adams, a young black man from Mantua who, in the late
1960s, took me along to a meeting in Chicago of prominent black leaders
from across the nation. The auditorium in which the meeting was held
was filled to the brim. I was one of only two whites who were there.
I sat in the back row with Forrest to minimize my conspicuousness.*

*The meeting was opened by Floyd McKissick, a well-known militant
black leader. While making his opening remarks he noticed me sitting
in the back row. He stopped, pointed at me, and demanded, "What's
that honkie doing here?"*

*Forrest jumped to his feet and, with all eyes focused on him, slowly
scanned the entire audience. When he had finished he yelled back to
McKissick, "I don't see no honkie here."*

That ended the matter. The meeting proceeded as intended.

**MORAL: Color is in the eye of the beholder, not in
the skin of the beheld.**

Those who genuinely desire to end discrimination seldom
know how to do so. They incorrectly view it as a gap between
us and *them* that can and should be bridged by symbolic acts.
Those on the far side of the gap are seldom taken in by such
gestures, however well intentioned they may be. The only way
to end discrimination is to close the gap, not bridge it. Bridging

the gap accepts the existence of two sides and the space that separates them.

🐝 🐝 🐝   I'm Not Your Brother

Two members of Columbia University's faculty phoned me in the early 1970s and asked for a meeting with Herman Wrice and me. The two professors were part of a Columbia group that, several years earlier, had received a large grant from the Ford Foundation to support self-development efforts in Harlem. The Columbia group had used all the funds with little, if any, effect on Harlem. Several executives of the Ford Foundation, who had recently visited Herman and me and observed our modest successes in Mantua, asked the two Columbia professors to visit us in order to find out why we were succeeding where they had failed.

The two members of the Columbia faculty arrived at my office as arranged. They were young and were wearing the uniform of the time: well-worn dungarees, sneakers, and denim jackets. They were bearded and long haired.

We chatted for a while, waiting for Herman. When Herman arrived, one of the Columbia professors jumped up, grabbed his hand, shook it vigorously, and said, "Hello, Brother."

Herman withdrew his hand quickly, backed up and said, "Don't you call me Brother!"

The Columbia professor was taken aback by Herman's reaction. He collected his wits and asked, "Why? Don't you let any white man call you Brother?"

Herman replied, "I do. One."

"Who's that?" asked the professor.

"Him," Herman replied, pointing to me.

"Why him?"

"Because he has enough sense not to try."

MORAL: A friend in need may not be a brother in deed.

It was from this episode that I learned what "brother" means to disadvantaged urban blacks, and why it is wrong for a white person to use it in addressing a black. Two disadvantaged blacks coming from the same ghetto share a feeling of alienation from society resulting from their segregation and being discriminated against. This is a feeling few whites—certainly not white Anglo-Saxon Protestants—can have in the United States. On the other hand, two blacks from the same ghetto may never cooperate in trying to improve conditions in their ghetto, as Herman and I have. Herman and I are colleagues and friends, but not brothers, and we can't be until discrimination against members of his race has ended and they have attained equality with members of mine.

I'll settle for being thought of by Herman as a friend rather than a brother. A friend is one you can trust to act in your interest even when doing so involves sacrificing his or her own personal interests. After all, Cain and Abel were brothers, not friends.

It is because of our differences, not similarities, that I am able to help Herman. I can provide him with some of what he needs, but I can't share his sense of oppression and alienation. On the other hand, because he is so different from me, I learn a great deal from him.

Closing the Gap

The longer the distinction between *us* and *them* has been maintained, the more difficult it is to close the gap it produces. The reduction of the very large gap that once separated Herman and me took several years to remove.

The problems associated with the black ghettos in urban America are familiar to most of us. Perhaps less familiar are the numerous unsuccessful attempts that have been made by many urban universities to contribute to the solution of these problems. It was awareness of most of these failures that in 1967 led my colleagues, professors Robert B. Mitchell (city planning) and William Gomberg (industrial relations), and me to engage in a discussion of the reasons for them. Out of this came a formulation of a very unconventional way for a university to try to help a black ghetto develop.

Our approach was based on a few simple assumptions. First, we assumed that inhabitants of black ghettos should be given opportunities to solve their own problems in their own way; that they should not accept white solutions because whites have not demonstrated any competence in solving black problems. Furthermore, we believed that blacks could extract more learning and development from their own failures than from white successes. Therefore, we concluded that the best way to help the black community was to provide it with (1) an opportunity to solve its problems however it wants to and (2) any assistance it wanted that we were able to provide. Our task and that of the university, as we saw it, was to make ourselves and our resources available to the black community to use as it, not we, saw fit.

An opportunity to try out our ideas arose when Forrest Adams, whom none of us knew at the time, came to us with a request for assistance in preparing a housing proposal to be submitted to Philadelphia's city government. The neighborhood from which he came, Mantua, covers about 80 city blocks and has a population of about 22,000, 98 percent of whom are black. It was a critical poverty area. Almost 25 percent of its housing units were overcrowded and more than 50 percent of them were in substandard condition. Its male unemployment rate was more than three times that of Philadelphia as a whole. There is no end to the statistics of degradation that could be cited.

We three professors arranged to provide Forrest with the help he wanted, but asked if he could arrange for us to meet with the principal leader in Mantua. Naturally, he wanted to know why. We said we had a proposition to make to that leader. Forrest asked us to tell him what our proposition was and he would convey it to the leader. Then, if the leader was receptive, Forrest said, he would arrange the meeting we wanted. We said we didn't want to do it that way because we didn't think our proposition would be credible if presented by anyone other than ourselves; it might not even be credible when we presented it. Forrest's curiosity was aroused by this. He said he would see what he could do.

The next day Forrest appeared with Herman Wrice, whom none of us knew at the time. We told him we had received a grant from the Anheuser-Busch Charitable Trust, as we had, that would enable us to employ three people from Mantua for nine months. These people, to be selected by Herman, would work on neighborhood development projects of his and their choosing, not ours, and report to him. We would exercise absolutely no authority over them; only he would be able to do so. Second, we three would be available to try to help the Mantuans selected in any way they requested, but we would do absolutely nothing on our own initiative. If the Mantuans made a request we were not able to handle, we would try to find someone who could.

Herman said that our proposition appeared to him to be a request for his community to teach us how to help it, to be an experiment that they would conduct on us. He understood us completely. Nevertheless, he wanted us to be sure we understood that we might never see those he employed and might never know what they were doing. We assured him that we were aware of this possibility but hoped it would not be realized.

Herman accepted our proposition and brought the three Mantuans he wanted to employ—Andy Jenkins, Dick Hart, and Doris Hamilton—to see us the next day, a Friday. He asked us to review the conditions of employment with them and give them a chance to question us about them. Among other things, we agreed to mail their paychecks to them so they would not have to come to us for them. Because of such concessions we survived their inquisition. They signed on.

On the following Monday morning the three of them were waiting for me when I arrived at my office. They said they wanted us to review their initial and tentative plan of activities, which they had developed over the weekend. When they began their review, their real reason for wanting it became clear: they identified more than 20 things they wanted us to do for them, things that were either difficult or impossible for them to do for themselves. For example, they wanted 500 gallons of dirty pond water for an aquarium they had installed in one of the neighborhood's schools. They also wanted us to get some cooperative action from the city's director of recreation. We said we would try to fill all their requests, but we could not promise success. They arranged to meet with us the next Monday to review our progress.

By the following Monday, much to our surprise, we had been able to fill most of their requests, but they were ready with a batch of new ones. The Monday-morning meetings were soon regularized, and the frequency of ad hoc meetings increased over time. It rapidly became apparent that we needed a full-time member of the university to work with them and coordinate all the work expected of us. This task was given to Marvin Rees, who until then had been the administrative officer of the research center I directed. Most of the credit for the accomplishments that followed belongs to him. Unfortunately, both he and Professor Gomberg have since died.

Six months after initiation of our joint effort, the Mantuan team members and we collaboratively prepared a proposal directed at obtaining increased and continuing financial support of our joint efforts. This proposal was submitted to both the Anheuser-Busch Charitable Trust and to the Ford Foundation. Anheuser-Busch provided us with funds sufficient to cover the next two years. It has supported this effort ever since. We also received a Ford grant, but Mantua and we were unwilling to accept Ford's stringent accounting requirements and had to turn it down. These requirements were suitable for a for-profit corporation, but not for a not-for-profit neighborhood development effort.

A very large number of development programs were introduced into the community, most of them successfully implemented and carried out. These included establishing:

- ❦ an industrial park that nurtured black small businesses and employed a number of Mantuans

- ❦ an employment service that helped Mantuans find jobs out of their community

- ❦ a credit union

- ❦ an Architectural and Planning Center that implemented about $6 million worth of development projects

- ❦ an agency for rehabilitation of old housing and construction of new ones

- ❦ a consulting activity directed at solving racial problems in government and industry, and an emergency task force, on call by the governor, for handling racial crises in the state of Pennsylvania

- ❦ an extensive educational program from infancy to junior college and a program in business education conducted collaboratively with and at the Wharton School

- ❦ competitive sports programs in every major and many minor sports involving up to a thousand young people, which frequently transported the young people involved to communities far from Philadelphia to compete

- ❦ day-care services for infants and young children

- ❦ health-care services within the community, which previously had none

- ❦ a drug-addiction treatment center and a city-wide war on drugs—a war that has received state and national attention.

This list is far from comprehensive. Because of these accomplishments, Mantua and Herman have received numerous local, state, and national awards.

Our joint effort continues after more than 20 years, during which Herman Wrice left Mantua for a while to direct an alcohol and drug rehabilitation center in Iowa and I retired from the university. Neither of these discontinuities interrupted our collaboration and friendship.

Trust

The essence of my friendship with Herman is mutual trust. Mutual trust does not develop easily between *us* and *them* because it is a product of what people do rather than what they say. The antidiscrimination rhetoric that bombards us in the United States belies the large amount of continuing discrimination. To be sure, there has been significant progress, but the progress that remains to be made is much greater than that which has been accomplished to date. How many whites and blacks interact socially? How many close black friends do whites have, and vice versa?

🦫 🦫 🦫   *It Don't Matter No More*

Immediately after the Ford Foundation made a substantial grant to Mantua and my university-based research group for continuation of our collaborative development effort (and before we turned it back), Ford issued a press release about the grant. KYW, a local television station affiliated with NBC, came to the Penn campus to interview Andy Jenkins, one of Mantua's development planners, and me for the evening news.

The interviewer asked Andy, "When the collaboration between Mantua and the Busch Center at The Wharton School first started, what did you think they were up to?"

Andy answered, "I had no idea, and I was very suspicious because the university had screwed us many times in the past."

"Now that you've been working with the people in the Busch Center for some time, what do you think their motivation is?"

"I still don't know, but it don't matter no more."

MORAL: Trust comes from the heart, not the mind.

My friend Dr. Morris Chafetz, president of the Health Education Foundation and one of the few sensible national voices on the subject of alcohol use and abuse, was once asked by someone who wanted to discredit his support of responsible drinking, "Don't you receive support from the brewing industry?"

Morris replied, "Yes, I do, but not enough."

What a wonderful response! It was so much better than to have apologized or excused himself for accepting such assistance. In effect, he said, "I am a professional, and as such I have standards to which I adhere. I would not tell a patient, even one who pays for my services, something that is not true even if he wants to hear it. Nor would I publish research results that I could not support adequately. Who supports my research is not relevant; the findings are."

Professionals who work on problems of social significance are frequently subjected to questions concerning the sponsorship of their work. The assumption that usually underlies such questions is that the sources of a professional's support impose their biases on that professional. Support from Anheuser-Busch is not provided for the purpose of inducing those supported to buy Anheuser-Busch products. Professional researchers can survive abandonment by sponsors who disapprove of their results, but they cannot survive professionally if a sponsor-imposed bias is revealed.

I once talked to a group of officials of the Teamsters union, trying to get them to agree to a cooperative effort with management of a company whose hourly-paid employees they had organized. One of the officials asked me who was paying for my time. I said the company's management was. He then asked why he should trust me. I answered that he shouldn't, not because I was being paid by management but because he had no reason to do so. I invited him to test me to determine if I was trustworthy or not. It was his duty, I argued, to conduct such tests and not to assume without supporting evidence that I was either biased or not. I argued that he could not afford to dismiss the possibility that I could be trusted because, if he trusted me, I would be able to help him attain many of his objectives.

☙ ☙ ☙   *Testing Trust*

In the early days of our work with Mantua I was frequently asked by people from that neighborhood why I should be trusted, particularly since the university of which I was a part was untrustworthy. Here, too, I told them there was no reason why they should, but why not test me in action? They did.

One day several Mantuans came to my office to ask a favor of me. There was an intersection in their neighborhood at which there were frequent collisions of automobiles. There had been about a dozen serious accidents on that corner in the last year. People who lived near that intersection had repeatedly asked the city to place signal lights at the corner, but to no avail. Therefore, they said, they had decided to put up their own lights. They intended to use coffee cans and Christmas tree bulbs attached to telephone poles located on each of the corners of the intersection. What they did not know, they said, was how to wire the lights and their controls. They wanted me to help them find out how to do so. I said I would contact some faculty members in the college of electrical engineering and try to get their help.

Before they left, I asked them what reaction they expected from the police when they began to put up the lights. They said the police were likely to take the lights down. I asked what they thought would happen while the police were doing this. They said a crowd would probably gather and bait the police. I asked if they thought this might start some serious trouble. They said it was likely. Then I suggested that, before they try to put up their own lights, they give me a chance to try to get the city to install legal ones. If I didn't succeed, I said, I would get them the wiring diagram they wanted. They agreed.

Fortunately, I was able to talk the city into providing the lights. After they were up, those who had made the request of me confessed that they had never intended to put up their own lights. They had wanted only to see if I would help them do something of which they thought I would disapprove because, they said, it was probably "slightly illegal." Apparently I passed the test.

MORAL: Trust is not a gift from others, it is compensation for work done.

Nonracial Discrimination

Race, of course, is not the only basis of discrimination in our and other developed Western societies, although it may be the most prevalent. Religion probably runs a close second, second because it is more difficult to identify one's religion than one's race by appearance. However, this difficulty is greater for some than for others.

❦ ❦ ❦   *The Tearing of the Green*

In the early 1980s I was working on the Northern Ireland government's executive development program. I would visit there periodically to give a series of lectures. My hosts were two senior members of the responsible department of the government. They and I became close friends. We frequently discussed the Protestant-Catholic problem confronting their country and what might be done about it. We even tried to do something about it, but government officials prevented us from implementing so much as the first step of our plan.

One day as I was going to a session attended by a number of high-ranking government officials with one of my two friends, I told him that I could not understand how the conflict between Catholics and Protestants in Northern Ireland could be maintained when it was impossible to distinguish between Catholics and Protestants by sight. Nonsense, he said; it was easy to tell them apart. Every Northern Ireland Protestant could spot a Catholic a mile away, and vice versa. I said I didn't believe him.

To settle the issue, he bet me that he could identify the Catholics in the meeting we were about to attend. (He had previously told me he knew only a few of those who were going to attend.) We agreed that, once he had made his determination, I would check its validity by asking for the truth from the government's personnel officer, who had arranged the meeting and had access to the personnel records of all those in attendance.

*When we entered the room I was introduced to each of the approxi-
mately 30 who were present. Meanwhile, my friend scanned the room.
Later, when we were seated, he whispered to me that there was only
one Catholic in the room, and he pointed him out to me. After the
meeting, with the help of the government's chief personnel officer, I
was able to determine that my friend was absolutely right. The one
Catholic present was the mayor of Londonderry.*

> **MORAL: When a distinction, however difficult to
> make, makes a significant difference, we learn how
> to make it.**

When I told this story to an old Catholic friend of mine back
in the States, he said, "Of course." He explained that he had
been raised in an all-Catholic neighborhood in South Philadelphia. At that time, when young male Catholics strayed into a
Protestant area or a young male Protestant strayed into theirs,
a violent reaction was likely. This being the case, he said, one
learned at an early age how to distinguish visually between
Catholics and Protestants. Survival depended on it.

When my army unit was shipped to the Pacific during World
War II, we had great difficulty distinguishing visually between
the Filipinos and the Japanese. Nevertheless, when we invaded
the Philippines our survival depended on our ability to make
that distinction. We rapidly learned how to make it.

Those who cannot see religious differences and for whom such
differences are important can always ask, but asking doesn't
always work.

❦ ❦ ❦   ***As In Politics, the Question Answered
May Not Be the Question Asked.***

*For a while my family and I lived in a small housing development just
outside of Cleveland. Our house was located about a hundred yards*

from the access road. Our mailbox was located at the junction of our driveway and the access road.

One Sunday morning as usual, I went out to my mailbox to collect the newspaper. One of my neighbors, generally reputed to be the development's principal snob, pulled up beside me in his car, said hello and asked, "Are you just coming from church?"

I said, "No."

He then asked, "When you do go to church, which one do you go to?"

I replied, "I don't go to church."

"Oh," he said, "then I suppose your wife takes the children to church. When she does, which one does she go to?"

"I don't know," I said. "I never asked her."

He drove off without another word.

> **MORAL: Few things are as uplifting
> as a good put-down.**

Snobbery, hence discrimination, does not require an important distinction to serve as its basis; it can rest just as well on one that is trivial.

❦ ❦ ❦   ***Put This in Your Pipe and Smoke It***

Until recently I was a very heavy pipe smoker. I smoked a pipe steadily for almost 50 years. Like most inveterate pipe smokers, I settled on a favorite brand early in my career and never strayed from it for long. I preferred a plain, ordinary, unperfumed tobacco. I thought fancy brands and specially formulated tobaccos were most likely to be smoked by infrequent or new smokers. Long-time pipe smokers realize that brand preference is a very personal matter, hence they seldom try to impose their tobaccos on others. On the other hand, new or light pipe smokers frequently insist that others try their tobaccos.

In 1942, shortly after I started to smoke a pipe, I was inducted into the army. By then I had experimented with several brands of tobacco and had not yet settled on the one that was to become my regular brand. I was smoking a blend produced by a Philadelphia tobacco company. It turned out to be impossible to find it in either army PXs or the drug stores in the communities near which I was stationed. Therefore, I imposed on my parents by having them mail a large tin to me periodically.

One day I was sitting in my tent in California's Mohave Desert puffing away on my pipe when my company's supply sergeant came in. He sat down, pulled out his corn-cob pipe, and began to fill it from his pouch. While he was filling his pipe, I began to empty mine. He offered me some of his tobacco. I took his pouch, filled a fresh pipe, and began to smoke it. His tobacco was by far the best I had tried up to that time. I asked him for its brand name and where he got it. He told me he ordered it from a tobacco factory in his hometown. I asked if it would be possible for me to do the same. He said it would. When I asked how to go about it, he said he would place the first order for me. I offered to pay him in advance but he said he preferred to wait until the tobacco was delivered. I was a bit apprehensive because the cost might be too high, but I agreed.

Several weeks later he brought to me a white muslin sack that held two pounds of tobacco. It was unlabeled and closed simply by a knotted drawstring at the top. When I asked the sergeant how much I owed him for the tobacco, he named an amount that was only a small fraction of what the same amount of my tobacco cost. I thought he might have made a mistake and ordered a different tobacco than the one I had tasted earlier, so I opened the sack and tried a pipeful at once. It was as good as I remembered. I asked the sergeant why the tobacco was so cheap. He said it was because the tobacco was the sweepings off the floor of the factory.

My snobbery based on product preference stopped right then. But I suspect that my snobbery based on the absence of such snobbery began at the same time.

❦ ❦ ❦

Many years later my friend Ed Vogel, who was vice president of marketing at Anheuser-Busch, started sending me rare and expensive pipe tobaccos specially mixed at Dunhill's in New York City. Although he did not smoke a pipe, he liked the odor they gave off.

I found the first pound of tobacco he sent to me intolerable, but of course I did not tell him that; I thanked him for the gift and told him how much I appreciated the rare blend. Ed said he would be going back to New York shortly and would get another pound for me. He asked how I would change the first pound to make it even more enjoyable. I gave him a few modest suggestions. The next pound arrived shortly thereafter and, although it was a bit better, I did not like it enough to replace the brand I smoked regularly. I gave Ed's tobacco away to a new pipe smoker who was sufficiently impressed by the tobacco's packaging and source to ignore its taste.

This sequence was repeated several times before Ed and I went to New York together. When we did, Ed suggested that we go to Dunhill's so that I might instruct them as to exactly the tobacco I wanted.

We went to Dunhill's in the Radio City complex, where a young man, certainly not more than half my age, came to take care of us. Ed explained the situation and gave him the number of the last tobacco "prescription" he had had filled. The young man retrieved my file and asked me what my preferences were. I told him I preferred an un-adulterated Kentucky burley. He then asked what brand I normally smoked. I told him Sir Walter Raleigh. The young man drew himself up to his full height and, looking down at me, said that Dunhill tobaccos were not meant for anyone so undiscriminating as to smoke Sir Walter Raleigh regularly. We left Dunhill's tobaccoless and stopped at a nearby drug store, where I bought another packet of Sir Walter Raleigh.

MORAL: There are only two kinds of snob: the kind others think we are and the kind we think they are.

There are those for whom products are status symbols. Possession of these products is believed to say something admirable about those who have them. Certainly a lot of advertising tries to make people believe this is the case. Snob appeal is a powerful motivating force. For example, as I write this, Harvey sherry is being advertised on television with a commercial in which one woman says of the product that it is "upper crusty." Snobbery is also responsible for the recent rash of designer labels that appear conspicuously on clothing and accessories.

Snobbery derives from a sense of superiority usually based on something for which the snob has no responsibility—for example, inherited wealth, social status of parents, or national origin. This is why the snubbed often fail to acknowledge the superiority of the snob. When those snubbed act as though the snob were really superior, it is usually to get something they, the snubbed, want from the snob.

It seems to me that snobs seldom suffer because of a lack of recognition of their assumed superiority by others. It is their feeling toward others, rather than the feelings of others toward them, that is the source of the superiority they assume.

Those afflicted with the we-they syndrome frequently assume that everyone is a member of one of these two categories, that they are exclusive and exhaustive. This can lead to unexpected results.

❦ ❦ ❦   *On Fine Distinctions*

After my experience regarding the ability of the Northern Irish to distinguish visually between Catholics and Protestants, I asked my Northern Irish friends how those who were neither Catholic nor Protestant fared in their country. In response I was told the following story:

A band of masked IRA gunmen came into a department store in downtown Belfast around noon, called for the owner, and demanded that he empty the store because they intended to blow it up. The owner was greatly distressed and protested, "I'm neither Protestant nor Catholic. I'm a Jew."

The leader of the band then asked, "Yes, but are you a Catholic or a Protestant Jew?"

> **MORAL: To the fanatic there is only one belief
> possible other than his own, and it is
> necessarily wrong.**

When discriminators are confronted by someone whose position they cannot classify, they are frequently thrown into a tizzy. Moreover, they resent the one who is an exception to their rule. They would much rather destroy, discard, or ignore the exception than deal with it. For them, one must be a member of either *us* or *them*.

☙ ☙ ☙   *Tao*

In 1936 a high school friend and I went together to register for our freshman year at the University of Pennsylvania. We were given a number of forms to fill out. One of the blanks to be filled on one of the forms was labeled "Religion." This struck us as odd since the university was nonsectarian. We asked a clerk why it was included. She said it was used to notify the appropriate chaplain in case of an emergency. My friend decided that discretion was the better part of valor and, rather than not respond, entered "Taoism" as his religion.

When we handed our forms to the clerk, she checked to see what we had done with the religion entry. When she came to Taoism, she asked my friend what it was. He said it was his religion. She said she had never heard of such a religion. He said he was sorry but that was not his fault. He added that there were probably more Taoists than members of the religion to which she subscribed. She took offense at this and instructed my friend to wait while she called her supervisor. When he appeared she showed him the Taoism entry and asked if it was acceptable. The supervisor said there was no such religion. My friend once again asserted that there was and suggested that the supervisor consult the university's professor of religion. The supervisor picked up the phone and did just that. The professor at the other end confirmed the existence of Taoism. The supervisor was very angry. He told my friend that he didn't believe he was a Taoist but that he had no time to investigate the matter. Therefore, he would have to accept the entry.

The next semester when both of us returned to register the same item appeared on our forms. This time my friend entered "Zoroastrianism." We turned in our forms to the clerk with whom he had had the encounter the previous year. She remembered him and, therefore, immediately turned to his religion entry. When she came to "Zoroastrianism" she looked up and took on the countenance of a cat that had just caught a particularly elusive mouse. She went to her files and withdrew my friend's previous form and confronted him with the fact that he had entered "Taoism" on the last occasion and now "Zoroastrianism." She demanded an explanation. My friend said he had been converted.

Unimpressed, she summoned the same supervisor she had summoned the previous semester. Once again he insisted there was no such church. My friend said there was. The supervisor, recalling the previous occasion, called the professor of religion and, much to his chagrin, learned that there was such a religion. Again he said he did not believe my friend but, although he had the inclination, he did not have the time to prove it.

My friend went through a religious conversion every semester he attended the university.

> MORAL: Although our society allows one to choose
> one's religion with absolute freedom, it does not
> allow one to choose "no religion" nearly as freely.

Segregation

Discrimination is often accompanied by segregation. The more segregation there is, the more difficult it is to eliminate discrimination. Recognition of this motivated the program for desegregation of schools in the United States, the objective of which was the elimination of discrimination.

We tend to think of segregation with respect to neighborhoods or housing, but, of course, it can take place in very small areas—for example, within buses or buildings. Executives occupy luxurious offices on the top floor while lower-level workers occupy open areas or Spartan offices on lower-level floors. This is a form of segregation and discrimination. Executive dining rooms and company planes are also instruments of segregation. Not too long ago I lectured to a military unit in an auditorium in which the highest rank sat in the front section and successively lower ranks sat in successively more remote sections. All such segregation is rationalized at least as fully as racial or religious segregation in society, but unlike segregation at the societal level, those who benefit from segregation within organizations cannot absolve themselves of responsibility for it.

It is sometimes easier to change segregation than discrimination, but it is seldom easy. To segregate is to separate physically; to discriminate is to separate mentally, and minds are harder to change than bodies. However, when segregation is abolished, discrimination is seldom far behind.

❦ ❦ ❦   *Squaring a Circle*

One of the principal manufacturing sites of a major corporation was scheduled to be shut down gradually over the next few years. The multiplant site had been unprofitable for some time. Corporate management blamed its poor performance on continuous labor-management problems. It was thought to be easier to withdraw than to beat one's managers against a union wall.

My university-based research group was called on by the site manager to help in an effort to make the plant viable and reverse the corporate decision to close it. Preliminary studies showed that unless the labor-management problems were solved, the plant could not and should not survive. This discouraged the managers at the site, because they believed it would be impossible to obtain cooperation from the hourly-

paid work force and its union. Nevertheless, we convinced the site manager to allow us to try to enlist the union in a cooperative effort directed at keeping the plant open. He arranged for us to meet with the executive board of the union. We were able to convince it to meet with the plant's managers to explore the possibility of cooperation— provided the union board could determine when and where the meeting would take place and how many from each side would attend. Management accepted this condition.

We asked the hotel designated by the union for a square or round room, one that had no head or tail to it. A square room was provided. Next, we wanted a round table capable of seating the 20 people who were to attend: nine from each side and two from the university. The hotel could not find a round table, so we settled for a square one.

Early on the morning of the first session my colleagues and I went down to check the arrangements. We placed name cards around the table, alternating union officials and managers. Each was flanked by the other. As soon as we were finished, two union officials came into the room and began to chat with us. One of them looked at the table and, without saying a word, went over to it and rearranged the cards so that all union members would be together on two sides of the table facing managers on the other two sides. When he was done and returned to the conversation, I went to the table and put the cards back in their original positions. The union official who had rearranged them looked at me, shook his head, and said, "It won't work." I told him it probably wouldn't but it was worth a try. He shrugged his shoulders, indicating he thought it was stupid to try.

A few moments later three managers came in and joined the conversation. One of them dropped out of the group, went over to the table and rearranged the name cards just as the union official had earlier. The union official laughed and explained his laughter to the puzzled manager. Meanwhile, I returned to the table and, once again, put the cards back in their original positions.

Eventually, all the attendees arrived and the meeting began. The attendees were obviously ill at ease because of the seating arrangement.

This put them in a bad humor, which was reflected in the fact that the entire first morning was spent with each side castigating the other.

I opened the afternoon session by reading an editorial from the company's newspaper about the union. It was vituperative and attributed to the union's leadership the worst of possible motives. We asked the managers if they really believed the editorial. With great embarassment the senior manager said, "No; it is exaggerated." I then read an editorial from the union newspaper. It was as hostile to management as the management editorial had been to the union. I asked the union officials if they really believed all the things said in the editorial. The president of the union said, "No; it, too, was exaggerated."

I then asked the managers and the union's officials why they permitted such deliberately inflammatory statements to be made. The answer was that "it was part of the game." I then asked if closing the site was part of the same game, and therefore something to be played but not taken too seriously. After some discussion, both sides assured me that it was not a game and that thereafter they would not treat it as such. Then they began to make tentative cooperative moves.

Over the next two days the sessions became increasingly cooperative. By the time we adjourned, they had designed a jointly sponsored Trust and Cooperation Program, which was implemented immediately. It turned that site's performance around completely and led to reversal of the corporate decision to close it. Today it is considered a model site.

I removed the name cards from the table before the third day's sessions began, thereby freeing the attendees to sit wherever they wanted. Each one took his originally assigned seat.

> **MORAL: Proximity is the mother of intervention.**

Conclusion

To discriminate is to make a distinction make a difference, and to use that difference to the advantage of the one who makes it. The distinction is normally based on a property of the discriminated over which they have no control, and which has no necessary effect on their ability to contribute to society's welfare. Moreover, the advantage to the discriminator is only apparent. There are hidden costs that outweigh the advantages. For these reasons, discrimination is irrational.

Nevertheless, discrimination is satisfying to many because it provides them with a sense of superiority; that it is not justified in fact is irrelevant. It is not surprising that those who have fewest objective reasons to differentiate themselves from most others are the most likely to discriminate.

Discrimination leads to underutilization of the potentialities of the discriminated, and therefore retards social development. That it retards the individual development of those discriminated against is obvious. Such retardation usually is brought about by reducing educational opportunities. The discriminators then mistake lack of education for lack of intelligence, the ability to learn. They also mistake a lack of hope for lack of motivation. Ironically, discrimination stimulates development of some capabilities among the discriminated that are sorely lacking among the discriminators, and the discriminators are blissfully unaware of this. Only those who can close the gap between *us* and *them* can share the learning that otherwise is exclusively *theirs*.

Chapter Five

Wisdom Is the Power to Put Our Time and Our Knowledge to Proper Use

People, Practice, and Professions

❦ ❦ ❦

Incomprehensible jargon is the hallmark
of a profession.

—Norman R. Augustine

I had an immense advantage over many others
dealing with the problem, inasmuch as I had no
fixed ideas derived from long-standing practice to
control and bias my mind, and did not suffer from
the general belief that whatever is, is right.

—Henry Bessamer

❦ ❦ ❦   *The Buck That Wouldn't Stop*

The vice president in charge of executive development in a large corporation once asked me to put on a two-day course for the top 200 executives of his company. He said he would like to have classes of only about 20 so there could be plenty of discussion. He placed the junior vice presidents in the first four sections, the intermediate-level vice presidents in the three following sections, the senior vice presidents in the next two sections, and the members of the executive office, including the chief executive officer, in the final session.

In the last meeting of the first class, one of the junior vice presidents said that, in his opinion, I was talking to the wrong group. He said he was very excited about what he had heard and that he would like very much to use it, but couldn't do so without the approval of his boss. Therefore, I should really be conducting the course at his boss's level. I explained that I would be interacting with his boss in a later class. He said he was glad to hear this and would approach his boss when they had both been through the course.

I had essentially the same exchange with someone in each of the first four classes. However, when I conducted the first class at the inter-

mediate level, the same statement was made by one of its members. He wanted to know if his boss, an executive vice president, would be similarly exposed to what he had heard. I said he would. Again, the same concern was expressed in each of the intermediate level classes. It was also expressed in each of the two senior vice presidential classes. I was asked if I would have a chance to expose the members of the executive office to what I had exposed them.

Needless to say, by the time I prepared for the class with the executive-office members I was curious about how they would respond. The answer came when the chief executive officer told me in the last session how much he liked what I had said and how anxious he was to apply it. However, he said, he would not be able to do so without the support of his subordinates, from whom he would like to receive a proposal for applying the material I had presented. Would I, he asked, get a chance to expose them to the same material?

> **MORAL: There is no better place for the buck to stop than with the person who has it now.**

Types of Professions

Professions, like organizations of any type, can be conceptualized in three different ways: as *input-defined*, *output-defined*, or *user-defined*.

Inputs, or functions, are services and products required by an organization to produce its outputs, whether they be goods or services. Put another way; the outputs of input-defined units are used or consumed within the organization. For example, the outputs of such input-defined units as automotive parts- and component-manufacturing divisions are used by those units that assemble automobiles. In corporations, some other typically input-defined units are finance, purchasing, data processing, maintenance, manufacturing, distribution, and personnel; in universities, academic, duplicating, records, admissions, placement, dining, student aid, and health departments are input-defined.

Outputs are the products or services that an organization makes available to entities external to it; for example, within General Motors the Cadillac, Buick, Oldsmobile, Pontiac, and Chevrolet divisions are *output-defined units*. Degree programs are output-defined units within universities; their products are professionals.

The outputs of output-defined units are inputs to *user-defined units* that make the organization's outputs available to the external world. User-defined units are usually said to be market-oriented. Users—consumers, customers, or clients—and units created to serve them are often classified geographically—for example, North American, Latin American, European, African, or Asian. They may also be defined by type of user—for example, manufacturers, wholesalers, retailers, government agencies, or ultimate consumers. Marketing units dedicated to selling products exclusively to each of these types of users are user-defined.

All three ways of dividing labor are used in most organizations, but labor is usually divided differently at different levels of the organizations. The primary orientation of an organization is determined by the principal criterion or criteria used to divide labor at the highest level of the organization. For example, if the units reporting to the chief executive officer of a corporation are defined by products, then the organization as a whole is said to be product-oriented.

All this about organizations is widely known. What is not well known is that professions are defined in exactly the same way. There are input-, output-, and user-defined professions, hence professionals, and there are very significant differences between them. (By *profession* I mean "an occupation or vocation requiring advanced study in a specialized field."[1])

Inputs are also whatever professionals use to do what they do professionally; for example, their tools, instruments, equipment, and techniques. X-ray equipment is an input to radiologists; the computer to software engineers; sampling and interviewing techniques to market researchers; chalkboards to professors.

Input-oriented professionals are ones defined by the inputs they employ. Radiologists, for example, are defined by the use of X-ray equipment, computer operators by the use of computers, pilots by the planes they fly, statisticians by the use of statistics, accountants by the use of accounting procedures, and so on. These are frequently referred to as tool- or technique-oriented specialists.

The problems, needs, and desires to which such professionals apply themselves are ones to which their defining inputs are believed to be applicable. Therefore, knowledge of the capabilities and limitations of their defining inputs is required to determine where best to use them. For example, use of radiologists is frequently specified by general practitioners of medicine.

Development of an input-oriented profession involves enlarging the set of instruments it uses and extending the uses to which its instruments can be put. Statisticians, for example, are continuously developing new sampling, estimating, and hypothesis-testing procedures and new applications for these and their earlier developed techniques. Such expansion and extension of uses can be dangerous if they tempt input-defined professionals to apply their instruments or techniques to inappropriate situations. There is an apocryphal story that illuminates this danger.

❦ ❦ ❦   *On Nailing Down a Problem*

The neighbor of an ardent do-it-yourselfer found him wandering through his house, a screwdriver in hand, obviously looking for some-

thing. However, what he was looking for was not obvious. The neighbor asked what it was.

"Loose screws," the do-it-yourselfer answered.

The neighbor said that this was a very inefficient way of making repairs. "Why don't you look for things that need fixing," he asked, "and then go to your shop in the basement and get the tools you need to do the job?"

"That would require too much upping and downing," the do-it-yourselfer replied.

The neighbor persisted. The do-it-yourselfer eventually became so annoyed with his neighbor that he agreed to follow his advice if he would get off his back. The neighbor agreed and the do-it-yourselfer went down to his shop. He returned a few minutes later with the same screwdriver in one hand and a file in his other, and he resumed his wandering search.

The curious neighbor followed the do-it-yourselfer and found that he was now looking for loose nails as well as screws. When he found one, he filed a slot in its head, inserted the screwdriver, and twisted it.

> **MORAL: There is more to solving an old problem than giving it a new twist.**

One way or another, input-oriented professionals must find or be given situations to which their instruments can be applied. For example, computer software engineers are continuously looking for new uses of computers and improving old uses. Universities, in which many faculty members are input-oriented professionals, have been characterized as places in which solutions can be found looking for problems.

Input-oriented professionals are much more interested in what problems have in common than in their uniqueness. Science in general is preoccupied with a search for what is common among things that are apparently different. The humanities, on the other hand, are preoccupied with looking for differences among things that are apparently similar. Because of this, the humanist is better at formulating problems than at solving them, and the scientist is better at solving them than at formulating them.

Humanists are more likely to get the wrong solution to the right problem, and scientists the right solution to the wrong problem. It is clear, therefore, that the integration of science and the humanities would be much more productive than their current separation. What we need is more of what might well be called the *scianities*.

Output-oriented professionals define themselves by the kind of situations they deal with, not how they deal with them, as do input-oriented professionals. Output-oriented professionals generally employ a wider variety of instruments than do input-oriented professionals, but contribute less to the development of the tools of their trades. The types of situations they deal with tend to remain relatively constant, but the instruments they use tend to vary over time. Examples of output-oriented professionals are those who produce compensation or incentive systems, management information, and automated office systems. Head hunters and auditors also fall into this category. In medicine, cardiologists, neurologists, urologists, and plastic surgeons are examples of output-oriented specialists.

Finally, *user-oriented professionals* are defined by the class of users they serve. They attempt to deal with as many as possible of the situations their users encounter. They define the class of problems with which they deal as broadly as their competence permits. Such professionals use a wide range of instruments and use a wide range of input- and output-oriented specialists. They are generalists. Like general practitioners of medicine, they treat whatever illnesses their patients may have. Pediatricians are output-oriented, since they serve whatever health problems young patients may have.

User-oriented professions tend to be more dynamic than the other types because the problems confronting their users change more rapidly than the instruments used to deal with them. They require continuous learning and do not require extended repetitions of the same kind of service. They are the least likely to deteriorate because of the changes required of them.

☕ ☕ ☕   *From Top to Bottom*

At the end of World War II, operations research (OR)—the application of scientific methods, techniques, and tools by interdisciplinary teams to managerial problems—emerged from under the cloak of military secrecy and entered the civilian world. It was especially welcomed by corporate executives preoccupied with the need to turn out more product less expensively. The desire for goods that had been repressed during the war asserted itself as soon as the war was over. Companies whose production facilities had been devoted largely to war production had to convert their old facilities and build new ones rapidly so as to get their share of the market that was out there waiting to be plucked. Operations research was admirably suited to serving those corporate executives who were so preoccupied; it was well equipped to handle the production-related problems that were at the center of their concern.

During the 1950s, operations research developed new tools, techniques, and methods that increased its ability to solve production-related problems. As a result, virtually every large American corporation acquired an internal operations research group. Most of them reported directly to chief executives or officers very close to them. At that time, operations research was user-oriented, taking on whatever problems executives and senior managers brought to it; the problems management brought to it were predominantly production-related and well suited to the methods, techniques, and tools OR employed.

By the 1960s American industry had built more than enough production capacity to meet consumer demands. Therefore, its principal problems changed to ones involving the creation of demand for the products it could produce. These were marketing and market-related problems. Operations research had difficulty dealing with such problems because the techniques and tools that had been developed for production-related problems were not as applicable to, or effective in, the marketing area. OR was confronted with a choice: develop new tools, techniques, and methods applicable to marketing problems and thus remain relevant to top management, or continue to work on predominantly production-related problems and move down the management scale to where these problems had been relocated. Most operations researchers chose the latter. They moved out of executive suites down to line managers' offices. The field became increasingly problem-oriented because it focused on the kinds of problems it knew how to solve, rather than on the kinds of problems the executives it had been serving now had to solve.

Meanwhile the tools, techniques, and methods that had been developed within, or for, operations research began to be taught in business schools and schools of engineering. Ability to use them was no longer restricted to operations researchers. As a result, the need for OR specialists further diminished.

By the seventies the markets for most products had been expanded to their limits. This meant that further corporate growth had to come from diversification and expansion of product lines and market areas. These problems, and the financial and strategic considerations on which they were based, moved into the focus of top management. Marketing problems moved down to middle managers, and production problems descended to the lowest level of managers. Courses in production management virtually disappeared in business schools. Operations research moved down the organization ladder with the problems to which it was stuck.

By the 1980s production problems were of low priority and the skills required for handling them were widespread and readily available. As a result, operations research was increasingly abandoned by its actual and potential users. OR turned inward and became increasingly introverted. It focused on its tools and techniques with little concern for their practical application. It hid this fact from itself by continuing to use the language of management that it brought with it during its emigration from the real world. Although this made it less suitable as an aid to management, it became more suited to academia, easier to teach. It settled in academia, where it was increasingly taught by people who had never practiced it and who had learned it from others who had never practiced it. The field became insipid, a diluted version of applied mathematics and statistics. Even a superficial glance at the journals published in the field confirms its increasing irrelevance.

MORAL: Continuous development of a profession and professionals requires at least as much concern with those they try to serve as with the means by which they try to serve them.

On Understanding Users

It is bad enough that most people believe they understand their own behavior; it is worse that they also believe they understand the behavior of others. When we ask ourselves or others why we or they do something, reasons are almost always provided. However, these reasons are more likely to rationalize than explain. One of my students once wrote that the reasons given for behavior seldom explain it; they "rationalies." He was righter than he knew. The lies, however, are not intentional; they are usually the product of ignorance. People just don't know why they do most of the things they do and why others do the things they do. They do not understand either themselves or others.

❦ ❦ ❦   *On Sweetness and Light*

In a study in which I was once engaged, I learned that the English consume considerably more sugar per capita than do Americans. I

*searched high and low for an explanation, but to no avail. In desper-
ation, I consulted a friend who was an executive in a sugar company.*

*When I asked him if he was aware of the fact that the English consumed
more sugar than we, he said, "Of course. Everybody knows that."*

*Rather than argue this point with him, I asked if he could explain the
difference.*

"Of course," he said. "The English like sugar more than we do."

*Again I restrained myself and did not point out that his answer was
tautological, which, according to Webster's New World Dictionary, is
"needless repetition of an idea in a different word, phrase, or sentence."
Rather, I asked, "How do you know they like it more than we do?"*

*He answered with a rhetorical question: "They eat more of it, don't
they?"*

> **MORAL: Some circles are much more vicious
> than others.**

This was clearly a case in which sweetness did not shed much
light. However, there are ways to gain understanding of users,
ways that do not involve use of questionnaires but do involve
either research on nonverbal behavior or user participation in
relevant decision making and design. In the sugar case, it took
a considerable amount of research to learn that the difference
in consumption is due to differences in protein-to-carbohydrate
ratios in English and American diets, and the greater amount
of physical activity in which the English characteristically engage. One would hardly expect an American, when asked why
he consumed less sugar than his English counterpart, to reply,
"For two reasons: The protein-to-carbohydrate ratio in my diet
is higher than it is in his, and he engages in more physical
activity than I do."

A material manufacturing company with which I have been
working recently told me that it takes two years or more to fill

a customer's request for a new or special material. When I asked why, I was told that, among other things, when the company develops a material that meets the customer's initial specifications and the customer begins to use it, he/she discovers that its specifications were not quite right. This starts a cycle of specification writing and material development that usually goes through several iterations before a satisfactory material is produced. This cycle reflects two facts: that the supplier has become an important part of the process of defining the customer's need and that the customer discovers the nature of his/her need or desire by engaging in the design of what he/she thinks will satisfy it.

🐚 🐚 🐚   *Toward Well-suited Men's Stores*

A chain of men's stores that sells a high quality of clothing at discount prices came to my research group for help in finding out why it was not attracting customers away from a particular competitive chain. Its managers told us they had interviewed a large number of these customers and had applied what they had learned from them, but none of this had had any effect on the chain's ability to attract these customers to their stores.

We arranged to have about 20 regular customers of the competitor spend a day with us designing their ideal men's store. They were not told who was sponsoring the study. The design they produced was incredibly creative; it differed from conventional men's stores in many significant ways. When their design was complete, we revealed the sponsor's identity and asked them to compare the store they had designed with those of the sponsor. This disclosed the principal reason for their not using our sponsor's chain, a reason that had never come out in the many interviews they had conducted. Our sponsor advertised the fact that it provided clothing of a high quality at the lowest prices available. The competitor's customers told us that when they want to buy clothing they decide on how much to spend before leaving home. Then they try to maximize quality for their predetermined price, not minimize price for a predetermined quality, which is what our sponsor offered to do for them.

> **MORAL: Asking is not always the best way to obtain an answer to a question.**

Most professionals have traditionally thought of themselves as experts who could provide those they serve with solutions to their problems. Physicians are the model. Patients come to them and present their symptoms; the doctors collect additional information, then diagnose and prescribe. In this model of professional service the recipients are relatively passive. It has become increasingly apparent, even in medicine, that recipients probably have more to do with solving their problems than do the professionals. Therefore, the role of the professional has come to be modeled more and more on that of the educator. This model is reflected in an ancient Iranian proverb that goes something like this: Give a hungry man a fish today and he'll be hungry tomorrow. Teach him how to fish and he'll never go hungry again.

The medical model of a profession applies reasonably well as long as the service rendered involves removal of a deficiency, getting rid of something the one served does not want—illness in the case of a doctor. However, professionals who are concerned with helping people get what they want or with helping them acquire the ability to get what they want necessarily focus on the way they and the recipients of their services *interact*, not how they act independently of each other. Increasingly, effective professionals do not act *on* their clients, but *with* them; they interact.

Participation and Development

Development, it will be recalled, was defined as: an increase in the desire and ability to satisfy one's own legitimate needs and desires and those of others. Because development requires motivation and learning and one cannot be motivated or learn for another, one person or group cannot develop another. However, one can encourage and facilitate the development of others; but this, as I pointed out earlier, can only be accomplished through the participation of the others. Therefore, all professional practice should involve the participation of all those who can be directly affected by the work of the professional, its *stakeholders*.

This requirement creates two problems. The first derives from the fact that all the stakeholders may not be accessible or, if accessible, may be too numerous to involve. The second problem derives from the fact that unless participation is voluntary, it cannot be effective. Consider each of these problems in turn:

It may be necessary in practice to use representatives of some of the stakeholders because of their number and dispersion—for example, a corporation's consumers or a university's alumni. Furthermore, a corporation's stakeholders include more than its consumers or customers. They also include its shareholders, creditors, debtors, employees, suppliers, the government, and the public. In some cases it may not be feasible to obtain the participation of representatives of a particular stakeholder group. Where this is the case, professionals have an obligation to represent the interests of the missing stakeholders as best they can. The focus of professionals should not be restricted to the interests of their clients; it should take into account the interests of all those who might be affected by what they do. In more than a figurative sense, all professionals are officers of society.

As a faculty member in various universities I have often felt it necessary to represent as best I could the interests of students and those who employ them upon their graduation. Faculties justify exclusion of students and other stakeholders from their deliberations on the ground that they, the faculty, know what the others need and desire and how to obtain it better than the stakeholders do. This justification is actually a rationalization of the fact that most faculty members don't care about what these stakeholders need and desire.

There is one stakeholder group, larger than all the others combined, that is usually completely ignored: future generations. If we believe in having stakeholders participate in making those decisions that affect them directly, how can we take into account the interests of the very young and those who have not yet been born? Clearly, it is not possible to represent them adequately. We don't know what their interests will be. Nevertheless, we can take into account one desire that we know they will have: the desire to make their own decisions.

Future generations should be allowed to decide for themselves. This requires us to keep their options open. We should not be making decisions that reduce the range of choices that will be available to them, but we continually do so. For example, destruction and pollution of the environment, extinction of certain species of wildlife, and exhaustion of limited natural resources clearly reduce future options. War is, perhaps, the activity that most restricts the options of contemporary as well as future men and women.

In many of our decisions we do not take into account our own future options, let alone those of others. For example, we construct buildings, bridges, highways, and all sorts of structures on the assumption that their use will not change over time. They are built rigidly and therefore are difficult to change. Yet there are few structures that are not significantly modified within a few years after their completion, and frequently modified thereafter. We know how to design and build structures that allow for almost unlimited changes at low cost and with minimal effort. Of course, such flexibility involves increasing their initial cost, but higher initial costs are usually more than justified by future savings.

Renewal of resources and flexibility of the artifacts that require them are keys to maintaining the options available to future generations. Assessments of future impact should be made of all decisions that have more than short-term consequences. Such studies should not differ much from environmental impact studies, except that they focus on stakeholders rather than the environment. Furthermore, these studies should be followed up systematically. Once the decisions based on such studies have been made, the predicted effects of these decisions on their stakeholders and the assumptions on which these expectations are based should be monitored closely and continually. Whenever either the assumptions or the actual effects of the decisions are observed to deviate significantly from what was expected, the relevant decisions should be reviewed and modified as required.

In my opinion, the freedom to decide, to make choices, is the most important freedom people of any age or Age can have. However, this freedom is empty without alternatives from which to choose. Therefore, to deprive future generations of options is to deprive them of their most fundamental right. Preservation of future options is an *ethical* as well as a developmental issue.

Ethics

Robinson Crusoe did not have to face any ethical issues as long as he lived alone on his island. Ethical issues arose only when his man Friday appeared. They arose because ethics has to do with the way people interact, not the way they act independently of each other. The number of interactions in which individuals, organizations, institutions, and societies are involved has increased dramatically with the explosive expansion of communication and transportation since World War II. As a result, ethical issues have become increasingly important, but our ability to deal with them has not increased proportionally.

"Ethics" and "morality" are usually treated as synonyms, but I prefer to think of ethics as having the function of *promoting cooperation*, and morality of *reducing conflict*, both with respect to legitimate needs and desires. Ethics, as I conceive it, is *prescriptive*; it tells us what should be done: thou shalt. I take morality to be *proscriptive*; it tells us what should not be done: thou shalt not. For me, good and evil are ethical concepts; right and wrong are moral concepts.

Good and evil and right and wrong are matters of degree; they are not dichotomies, not either-ors. To reduce conflict is right, but the amount by which it is reduced determines how right it is. Similarly, to increase cooperation is good, but the amount by which it is increased determines how good it is.

The systems philosopher C. West Churchman recently wrote:

> Morality is an endless conversation of the living with our ancestors about how to design a good world for future generations. And the conversation needs to be intelligent. . . . If one insists on a yes or no, the conversation ends. But it should not end. This means that a definitive yes or no never occurs: morality is neither absolute nor relative.[2]

Churchman's concept of ethical-moral judgments as continuing rather than final is very different from the traditional one. Ethicists and moralists have traditionally sought rules of conduct that enable us to make final good-evil or right-wrong decisions. The Ten Commandments, the Golden Rule, and Immanuel Kant's Categorical Imperative are examples. The authors of such rules reduce ethical-moral judgments to determinations of conformity to rule. This not only requires yes-no outputs of such judgments, but invariably gives rise to ethical-moral dilemmas. For example, who authenticates the rules? The answer has usually been God. Which one? What assurance do we have that those who claim to speak in His (or Its) name are authorized to do so? How do we account for the incompatibility of rules derived from belief in the same God, let alone different ones?

"Conscience" provides no better answers to such questions than "God." Whose conscience? How do we deal with conflicting dictates of different consciences? And so on and on.

No set of ethical-moral laws has yet been formulated that does not lead to unresolvable problems. This is true even of the Ten Commandments. For example, there are times when honoring one's parents and telling them the truth are in conflict.

I suggest a different approach to ethical/moral judgments: one based not on conformity to rules but on the way the judgments are made—on *process*, not *product*. Put another way, I believe that ethics and morality are not matters of *what* is decided but *how* it is decided. Definition of the ethical-moral decision process must answer two questions: Who should be involved in making a decision? and Of what should their involvement consist?

My idealized answer to the first of these questions is: All those who will be directly affected by a decision should be involved in making that decision. Therefore, whether we approach professional practice from the perspective of development or from the perspective of ethics, we come up with the need for stakeholder participation in decision making. This is not surprising because, in a very important sense, development is the ultimate good, hence the proper foundation of ethics. If an individual had the desire and ability to satisfy all his/her legitimate needs and desires and those of others, all other legitimate objectives would be attainable. Ethical and developmental pursuits are the same: the cooperation of people in their efforts to satisfy their legitimate needs and desires and to increase their ability to do so.

I have never encountered a conflict that was not resolved when the relevant parties were willing to sit around a table and discuss their differences. However, I have encountered conflicts in which the relevant parties were not willing to meet—for example, in Northern Ireland and in the Middle East. I have never heard what I consider to be a reasonable excuse for not meeting in an effort to settle differences. As a result, I tend to respond to conflicting parties that will not come to the table with an a-plague-on-both-your-houses attitude.

On occasion, I have been asked how I handle unresolvable conflicts. I point out that the question is meaningless: to say that a conflict is unresolvable is to conclude that it cannot be handled. Therefore, the assertion that there are unresolvable conflicts is a self-fulfilling prophesy. Most unresolvable conflicts are not resolved because the parties involved do not want to solve them, not because they can't be resolved. Those who classify conflicts as unresolvable unconsciously cooperate with those who are not willing to resolve their conflicts.

❦ ❦ ❦   *Immobilizing Conflict*

I once had a conversation with officials of a small nation that had experienced and continued to experience continuous conflict with all of its surrounding neighbors. I suggested that its situation could be significantly improved by moving the nation to another location and that this would be less expensive in the long run than maintaining its current position. When the officials objected to leaving a great deal behind, I said it would be possible to move all of their buildings as well as their people. Yes, they said, but the location and the land would be different. I suggested that we move, say, six inches of the topsoil so the land would remain the same. No, they said, the place would be different. I asked how much of the soil would have to be moved before the place was the same. They said I was missing the point; no depth would satisfy the requirement of making the place the same.

I asked how place was determined and they said by use of geographic coordinates. I then suggested we arrange for a change of the coordinate system so that their new location would have the same coordinates as their old one. No, they insisted, this would still not be the same location. I then pointed out that the only remaining characteristic that could define their location was the fact that it was surrounded by hostile neighbors and that this was the property of their location that they were most anxious to preserve. All other properties of their location could be reproduced or found in another place. The intensity of their response to this suggestion assured me that I had hit on the essential characteristic of their location.

MORAL: There is no way of resolving conflict between people who agree to disagree and who value that disagreement.

Inducing Participation

How is the voluntary participation of stakeholders in decisions that affect them directly most likely to be obtained? When they believe (1) the outcome of the decision will make a positive difference to them, (2) their participation can make a difference in the outcome, (3) participation will be fun, and (4) implementation of the results is likely.

The reason that most elections in the United States do not attract a majority of those eligible to vote is that the nonvoters do not believe their vote, or the outcome of the vote, will make any difference, because there is no significant difference between the opposing candidates. It was once said of our country that it makes no difference whom we elect as president. If he/she is good, the political system will reduce him/her to mediocrity. If he/she is bad, the political system will elevate him/her to mediocrity. The only elected officials who are not affected by the system are those who are mediocre to start with.

The belief that their participation can make a difference in outcome is strongest where the stakeholders have, and believe they have, an equal voice in decision making and the decisions are made by consensus. In turn, they are most likely to believe they have an equal voice in decision making when no single stakeholder group constitutes a majority of the decision-making body or, if one does, complete agreement among the decision makers is required. This precludes majority rule, hence a possible tyranny of the majority.

For me, consensus is a special kind of agreement, an agreement to act, an agreement *in practice* rather than an agreement *in principle*. The difference between practice and principle in this context is critical. This difference is illustrated by the following story:

❦ ❦ ❦   *Jim Rinehart*

Jim was chief executive officer of the Clark Equipment Company in the early 1980s. He was and is exceptional in many ways, one being his ability to generate consensus.

At one point he assembled about 70 managers at the top two levels of his corporation. He divided them into eight teams and sent them off for a day to produce a redesign of the corporation's structure. On the following day he had each team present its design to the entire group. After this was completed he announced that he was going to ask for a vote to determine which design the group liked best.

He asked those who thought the first team's design was best to raise their hands. About one-eighth of the people in the room did. The same thing happened on each successive vote. He clearly lacked a majority opinion. However, he had a consensus, one that was revealed by the answer to his next question.

Jim said to the group, "I'll give you the following choice: Either we keep the corporation's current structure or you let me pick at random one of the eight presented here." The vote was almost unanimous for Jim's random choice. However, when the group became aware of the fact that almost everyone in it preferred any of the designs to the one they currently had, they asked to go back into teams and see if they could synthesize the designs that had been produced into one that would be supported by consensus. Jim allowed them to do this and, eventually, they did reach a consensus design.

> **MORAL: When nothing can make things worse,**
> **doing anything makes them better.**

In my experience, complete agreement on what is the best decision is reached in about 75 percent of the decision-making situations involving groups. Where such agreement is not reached, the following procedures can be used to generate consensus:

First, formulate precisely the alternatives that have some support but not support from all. Second, collectively design a test of the effectiveness of the alternatives; this test should be acceptable by consensus and all should agree to abide by its results. Then conduct the test and implement its outcome.

❦ ❦ ❦　　　*Capital Punishment*
　　　　　　Is Not Necessarily Capital

During the 1975–1976 academic year that I spent in Mexico, one of the projects I worked on was very unusual. Mexico's secretariat of the presidency gave the university-based research group of which I was a part the funds required to run an experiment in a very underdeveloped community. The community selected was nested in the Sierra Madre

mountains about four hours by jeep from the closest highway. It con-
sisted of about 400 Indian families.

Approximately $40,000 in U.S. currency was deposited in the com-
munity's name in the nearest bank, which was several hours away.
The village was allowed to use this money only for development proj-
ects, and these had to be selected democratically in town meetings.

The community did not consider the government of Mexico to be
legitimate but considered it to have been imposed on the native Indians
by Cortes and maintained by Spaniards ever since. Therefore, it did
not accept the laws enacted by that government. It decided to prepare
its own legal code.

The question was raised as to whether or not the community should
apply capital punishment to those who committed capital crimes. There
was no agreement. At the town meeting in the town square at which
the issue was debated, I broke in and pointed out that there was complete
agreement on an important aspect of the issue. The villagers expressed
surprise at my statement and challenged me to identify the agreement.
I said that they all agreed that the village should minimize the number
of people murdered. They said, "Of course, but there is no agreement
as to how best to do this." I then pointed out that this was a question
of fact, and subject to objective settlement.

We then went about designing a retrospective experiment to test the
effectiveness of capital punishment as a deterrent to capital crimes in
the rest of Mexico. This was tricky, because no one could be killed in
the experiment. A consensus design was eventually reached. The vil-
lagers agreed to abide by the outcome indicated by the proposed re-
search, whatever it might be.

The states of Mexico were placed into four categories:

1. *Those that disallowed capital punishment up to five years ago*
   and continue to disallow it.

2. *Those that disallowed capital punishment up to five years ago*
   but have since instituted it.

3. *Those that used capital punishment up to five years ago and continue to use it.*

4. *Those that used capital punishment up to five years ago and have discontinued it since.*

Then the changes of incidence rates of capital crimes in the four categories prior to and during the last five years were analyzed. The analysis revealed that capital punishment had not deterred capital crimes in Mexico. The village then decided to disallow it.

MORAL: Opinion's most deadly enemy is fact.

Where consensus cannot be reached on the design of a test, or there is not enough time or resources available for conducting one, there is a fall-back or last-resort process. When the chairperson of the decision-making session feels that complete agreement cannot be obtained and that all the points of view have been expressed, he/she has each participant briefly summarize his/her position on the issue. Then the chairperson formulates the decision he/she will make if agreement among the other participants is not reached. The chairperson also commits him/herself to abiding by any decision the others agree on, even if it conflicts with his/hers. Once again, the chairperson calls on each participant to state his/her position briefly. Then, if any two or more of the participants disagree, they agree on the chairperson's position.

Participants in this procedure have always felt that it was both fair and necessary.

Fun

The best way I know of to make problem solving fun involves use of what I call *idealized redesign*. The participants in this process are asked to assume that the entity that has the problem they are trying to solve was destroyed last night, but everything else remains the same. Then they must redesign that entity so as to eliminate the problem that faces it. Their redesign is subject to only two constraints: first, it must be technologically feasible, and second, it must obey the same externally imposed constraints (e.g., the laws of the land) to which the current system is subject. In addition, it should be designed so that it can (1) improve itself by learning from its own experience, (2) adapt to a changing environment, and (3) be improved by being redesigned again in the future.

It is because the entity is designed with virtually no constraints that I call it idealized. However, the entity designed is never ideal or utopian because it is conceived so as to be able to improve itself or be improved by its designers over time. Therefore, the product of an idealized redesign is not a perfect, ideal, or utopian entity, but the best ideal-seeking entity its designers can currently imagine.

Idealized design enables those who participate in it to play God, because in this exercise they can create with virtually no constraints. They can be creative because such design is at least as much play as work. The conditions assumed are so unrealistic that the process cannot be treated as work, only as play. Because it is treated as play, creativity is unleashed and it is fun. Moreover, as the process develops it usually becomes apparent that the system designed can be attained or very closely approximated. In almost every case the principal obstruction between the designers and realization of their idealized design is *them*. As Pogo once observed: "We have met the enemy and he is us."

☙ ☙ ☙   *On Letting Go of Tenure*

At one time, the man appointed to the presidency of the university of which I was a part was an old personal friend. We met periodically for lunch to talk about old times and new. On one of these occasions he asked me to give him a frank opinion of how well he was doing as president. I hesitated, but he urged me to answer. I told him that from an academic point of view, the only viewpoint I could take with some justification, I thought he was doing a poor job or, more precisely, no job at all. He had not done anything but give speeches.

He responded defensively and said there was little he could do academically that would matter. He went on to explain. The principal problem of the university, he said, was the large number of tenured faculty members who were no longer productive researchers or effective teachers. The academic aspects of the university could not be significantly improved, he said, without removing and replacing them. Then, I asked, why didn't he remove them? He said they could not be removed because they were tenured. He pointed out that a tenured professor could be dismissed only on grounds that applied to few if any of the cases to which he referred. For example, a tenured professor could be dismissed for immorality or incompetence, allegations that, even if justified, were very difficult to prove.

I said I thought there were a number of other ways of getting rid of tenured professors. He said I was wrong, that I was out of my domain of competence and that further conversation along this line was a waste of time. He turned our conversation to another subject.

About a week later I sent him a memorandum identifying a number of ways that a tenured faculty member could be dismissed without use of difficult-to-prove grounds. He did not respond. A while later I ran into him entering the faculty club and asked if he had received my memorandum. Yes, he had. Then why hadn't he replied? Because, he said, I had completely missed the point. I asked what that point was.

"What would the faculty think of me and do to me if I did any of the things you suggest?"

Tenure was not the obstruction; his desire for approval of the faculty and fear of the possible consequences of their disapproval were.

MORAL: What others think of us is often more on our minds than theirs.

The reason most frequently given to me by managers and administrators for not doing something is that, although they would like to do it, their bosses would not approve. I have repeatedly found that most managers try to propose to their bosses only those actions of which they think their bosses will approve. In most such cases it is futile to point out that managers are not paid to make up their bosses' minds—their bosses are paid to do this—but to make up their own minds and expose them to their bosses.

Most people in positions of authority try to absolve themselves of responsibility for doing something that might be wrong. They do this by getting approval of a superior before acting. This absolves them of responsibility for error, passing it on to the one who approved their action, yet often leaves them in a position to claim credit for a correct decision.

I have often been asked: Where in an organization is the best place to initiate a new idea? The answer is very simple and should be obvious: Wherever you are. Unfortunately, we breed managers and administrators who are risk averse, who try to maximize their personal security. As a result, they act like nonprofessional employees rather than professionals.

Doctors employed by corporations do not try to get approval of their prescriptions for corporate patients before issuing them. They take responsibility for them; they have sufficient confidence in their ability to do so. Not so for most managers. Their mind-set is more like that of a servant than a professional. Business schools do not educate future managers to behave as professionals, only to claim professionalism.

Professionals must have clear ideas of the minimal conditions under which they are willing to conduct their practices. When these conditions are not met, they should refuse to practice and resign if necessary. The threat of withdrawal is the strongest protection a professional can have of his professionalism. However, this threat should never be made unless the one making it intends to follow through if the demands are not met.

✿ ✿ ✿   *Rejection without Resignation*

When I was a departmental chairman in a university, I twice recommended promotion of a particular member of my department's faculty. It was rejected by higher authority both times. I submitted my recommendation a third time and told the faculty member involved that I was doing so. He told me that he would resign if he did not receive a promotion this time, and that he intended to tell this to the dean. I asked him not to, saying I would convey that message to the dean. He asked why he shouldn't do so. I explained: If he told the dean he would resign and if his promotion were rejected, he would have no alternative but to resign. However, if I told the dean of his intention and the dean refused to promote him, he could say I had misinformed the dean and remain without loss of too much face. He agreed to let me do it.

I had to leave on a trip immediately following this conversation. The faculty member involved could not stand the delay and decided to see the dean during my absence. He told the dean of his intention to resign if his promotion were turned down, and the dean immediately said that he would accept that resignation. The faculty member was shocked and crushed. He phoned me and told me what had happened. He asked that I intervene because he did not really want to leave.

I managed to enable him to stay, but he never got the promotion he wanted and eventually did resign.

**MORAL: It is very dangerous for a sheep to pretend
to be a wolf.**

Friendship

Professionals cannot be very effective unless they are trusted by those they serve. Such trust is best exemplified by friendship. Friends are those whom we believe will act in our best interests even when doing so requires them to sacrifice their own interests. The probability of implementation of professional advice is directly proportional to the degree of friendship between the professional and the one receiving his/her service. We pay much more attention to advice received from friends than from acquaintances or strangers, and we get much better advice from them. However, it is often much more painful to receive.

❦ ❦ ❦   *Stafford Beer*

Stafford Beer, the eminent British management scientist and cyberneticist, is one of my old and valued friends. Although I have a great deal of respect for his work, I disagree with much of it and much of this disagreement is fundamental. When asked, as I frequently am, how I can maintain a close personal relationship with someone with whom I disagree so fundamentally, I point out that I have learned more from my disagreements with Stafford than I have from my agreements with many others. The reason our disagreements have never affected our friendship is rooted in an experience I had with Stafford many years ago.

When he wrote his book Decision and Control[3], *he sent a copy of the manuscript to me asking for suggestions and comments. I was torn by this request. As a friend, I felt obliged to comply, but I hesitated to point out all my disagreements with the content of the book because they might cost me his friendship. After some agonizing, I decided to share my unfiltered reactions to his book with Stafford. I sent him 13 pages of single-spaced typewritten criticism. In my covering letter, I described the agony I had gone through in preparing that letter.*

The response I received from Stafford was completely different from what I expected, but not different from what I should have expected. He wrote that he had never received such a demonstration of friendship as my letter. He thanked me for the time and effort I had put into preparing my criticism and comments. He even made changes in his manuscript consistent with many of them.

Since then we have been freely critical of each others' professional work without fear of retribution. After about 30 years of mutual disagreement, we are closer friends today than we were when all this started.

**MORAL: Wrongs are easily righted among friends,
and rights are easily wronged among enemies.**

My relationship with Stafford reflects a conversation I once had with another friend, Maurrie Creelman, a clinical psychologist in Cleveland, Ohio. I was about to become a father for the first time and my wife and I were as apprehensive as most prospective parents are about their ability to raise a child properly. I asked Maurrie if she could advise us. She said that if we kept one principle in mind we would not have to worry about parenthood. When a child does something bad, she said, never tell the child that he or she is bad; tell the child that what he or she has done is bad. Don't confuse what a child is with what a child does. Never suggest or imply that you are withdrawing your love of the child because of your disapproval of what the child has done.

Stafford was able to see my criticism as criticism of his work, not of him, and to accept it as evidence of my caring for him. He was right; I would never spend as much time and effort criticizing an enemy.

Care, not agreement, is the key to a person's heart.

❦ ❦ ❦   *Father and Son*

A company for which I had been doing research was in the process of bringing out a new product. It had introduced the product in two relatively unimportant states as tryouts and was about to introduce it in a third very large and very important state. I was asked to evaluate the plan for that introduction. My research indicated that the introduction could be improved significantly, but this would require use of unconventional and untried procedures.

The new procedure I recommended was widely and heatedly debated around the company. It was strongly opposed by some, including a few senior executives. However, support from the chief executive officer settled the issue in my favor.

Shortly after this decision was made, the brand manager of the product to be introduced had a massive heart attack and was forced to take an early retirement. On my recommendation, the son of the chief executive officer, a very promising and exceptionally capable young man, was moved into the vacated position. He had worked closely with me during my study of product introductions and therefore was very familiar with, and supportive of, the new procedure I had proposed.

However, once I knew of the young man's appointment, I asked for a meeting with his father, the CEO. At that meeting I suggested he withdraw the decision on the way the product was to be introduced in the next market and return to the conventional way of doing it. He was surprised by my suggestion and asked for an explanation. I said that because of his son's work with me and the belief by some managers that he had been promoted because of his relationship to the CEO rather than his ability, if the new procedure failed, he would be blamed for it. However, if it succeeded, he was unlikely to receive credit for it. Since I personally believed the son had great executive potential, I did not think his opportunity for advancement should be placed in jeopardy by the next step in the product's introduction. The new introductory procedure could be tried later in an area that was not as critical to the product's success.

The father listened carefully. Close to the end of my remarks he began to sob quietly. Embarrassed, he rose and left the room, mumbling, "You really care, don't you?" His attitude toward me completely changed for the better that day.

Later, the CEO did resurrect the earlier plan for the product's introduction, but the new procedure was subsequently used in the opening of additional markets. The son eventually became an outstanding senior executive, and he did so on merit and with the unanimous support of his peers.

MORAL: People are more important than anything.

That same father reacted very differently when he thought I did not care about the same son.

❦ ❦ ❦   *F--- You, Doc*

The corporation's senior marketing vice president had a serious dis-agreement with the son, who was then a junior marketing vice president; they disagreed on the maximum size of their principal product's inventory that should be maintained in the company's distribution system. The research group of which I was a part was asked to conduct a study to settle the dispute. It became apparent early in the study that the senior vice president was right and the CEO's son was wrong.

The son believed our research was biased in his superior's favor, so he employed a prominent consulting firm to look at the same problem independently. He hoped it would come up with a different finding. His hopes were transparent, so it was not surprising that the consultants obtained the result he wanted.

A meeting to resolve the differences between their research and ours was held in the office of the chief executive officer, the father. The CEO sat at the head of the table with his son on his immediate left. The son's consultants sat next to him. I sat at the foot of the table with the senior vice president of marketing on my right. Other senior executives, including the president, sat on the other side of the table.

I made our presentation first. The son's consultants followed. Because (1) they were not as familiar with the company and its products as we were, (2) they had less time to conduct their study than we, and (3) the conclusion they were to reach had been "suggested" to them, their work was significantly inferior to ours. As a result, it was easy to point out the deficiencies in their work. The son came to their defense and increasingly took responsibility for the mistakes they had made.

The chief executive officer became more and more uncomfortable as the weaknesses of his son's arguments were revealed. The discussion reached a point that he could no longer tolerate. He rose, leaned over his end of the table, glared at me, and said, "F--- you, Doc." He then turned and left the room in haste.

Those of us who were left in the room were stunned. The president broke the awkward silence by saying that no decision would be made at that time and adjourned the meeting. Everyone left in haste.

Fortunately, the disagreement was soon forgotten.

> **MORAL: If A loves B and C hates B, then A will hate C.**

Friendship is based on caring and caring rests heavily on respect. Respect cannot be demanded or taken; it can only be given.

❦ ❦ ❦   *Woods Hole*

A number of years ago the U.S. Department of Defense became seriously concerned about the continuing shrinkage of our Merchant Marine fleet. It was concerned because, in case of a war, we might not be able to control sufficient shipping to move what had to be moved to wherever it might have to be moved. Therefore, the department asked the National Research Council (NRC) to form a task force to seek a solution to the problem and suggest a future for the Merchant Marine. About 20 scientists, engineers, and transportation professionals were assembled. I was one of them. Admiral Arthur Radford, then joint chief of staff, agreed to chair the group, which convened at Woods Hole, Massachusetts. I was not an admirer of the admiral. To me, his much-publicized position on the use of nuclear weapons as deterrents to war was both irrational and very dangerous. I also thought he treated his opposition disrespectfully. This made it difficult for me to respect him.

Since the work of the task force was to extend over three weeks, we were invited to bring our families. Most of us did so.

I appeared at the appointed time and place for the opening meeting. All the task force members were there except the admiral. After we were all seated, he was announced by his adjutant and he entered the room. Everyone arose except me; I remained seated. When the adjutant gave the signal, the others sat down and the meeting proceeded.

Immediately after the meeting I was summoned by the adjutant, who told me that my failure to rise when the admiral entered the room was offensive to him. He said rising was a sign of respect for the man and his office. I explained to the adjutant that I did not respect the admiral, and that I did not want to behave hypocritically. Nevertheless, the officer told me, my continued failure to rise when the admiral entered the room could not be tolerated. Either I would have to agree to rise when he entered a room or I would have to leave the project. I told him I would pack and leave immediately.

I returned to the office that had been assigned to me and began to pack the few things I had unpacked earlier. While doing this, several other members of the task force stopped by to ask what had happened at my meeting with the adjutant. I told them. They were outraged.

They left my office and set about organizing a protest. They did so quickly and went to see the adjutant, whom they told that if I were permitted to leave they would also leave. A heated discussion followed. The admiral was consulted. He was more conciliatory than his adjutant. He agreed to being treated as other members of the task force, with no less or more deference than the others received.

As a result, I was asked to stay and I did. Fortunately, in the weeks that followed I was not required to interact with the admiral. In fact, he didn't interact with any of the members of the task force. He appeared only on ceremonial occasions.

On the evening of the last day of the task force, the admiral threw a beach party for its members and their families. I came with mine. Shortly after our arrival, my three-year-old son asked if he could meet the admiral, of whom he had heard me speak often. I said he could. I hoisted him up on my shoulders and went off in search of his highness. I found him surrounded by a group of task force members and their families. We worked our way up to him and I introduced my son. He responded graciously.

My son asked, "Admiral, are you in the army or the navy?"

The admiral laughed. My accumulated resentment against him was completely dissipated in that moment. I would have stood up the next time he entered a room I was in.

> **MORAL: Respect should be based on what a person does, and not on any other personal characteristic.**

The characteristics of a position or title that induces people to respect its occupant or holder is its uniqueness and the difficulty involved in getting it. Unfortunately, people can rise to respected positions without having any of the personal properties that we respect. Nevertheless, we are then expected to respect them because we do not know how to distinguish between respect for an individual and respect for the position he/she holds.

Degrees and titles, like uniforms, are better reflections of how their bearers feel about themselves than of how others feel about them.

Introductions

Formal introductions of an individual to an audience are frequently equivalent to putting a costume on that individual. They often distort the audience's perception of the individual introduced and, more importantly, that person's perception of him/herself. It can be embarrassing to listen to one's eulogy before one has died, and it can be very embarrassing to others if the person eulogized believes it.

Because I often give public addresses I am frequently subjected to excessively long and flowery introductions made by people who, in most cases, do not know me. I resent such introductions but feel that it would be unkind to strike out at the guilty party, who, after all, is trying to please me and impress the audience. Introducers do not realize audiences evaluate a speaker by what he or she says rather than what is said about him or her. To relieve myself of the resentment I feel after an extravagant introduction, I often open my remarks with, "After that introduction, I can hardly wait to hear what I have to say." The audience invariably gets the message, but, I find, the introducer seldom does.

I remember hearing of a case in which a speaker, after an excessively long and laudatory introduction, rose and said, "Anything I might say now would be anticlimactic," and sat down, refusing to say anything more.

The loudest applause I ever received occurred during a meeting at which the chairman had allowed the preceding speakers to run considerably overtime. I was introduced to the session, which was the last of the day, long after it was to have been terminated. I rose and said that under the circumstances I had no more interest in speaking than the audience had in listening to what I had to say, and sat down. The applause was deafening. The meeting was adjourned.

Many hosts are very insensitive to the value that speakers place on their time. Hosts may mean well, but they often impose their wills on visitors in thoughtless ways. For example, after agreeing to come to a university and give a talk in the morning, I learned when I got there that arrangements were made for me to speak again in the afternoon and evening. After all, they said, I was going to be there anyhow so I might as well be speaking.

It is not unusual to be told after one has delivered an invited lecture that a written version of the lecture is expected and that the host organization plans to publish it. This is frequently thought of as a favor to the speaker. The possibility that a speaker may prefer to use his/her time in other ways does not enter the minds of those who have such expectations.

Bertrand Russell is reported to have reacted to an expectation of others in a way I have always wished I had the nerve to imitate.

❦ ❦ ❦   *Food for Thought*

Russell was invited to deliver a lecture at a university in a city other than the one in which he lived. He agreed to do so for a fee. He was asked what his fee would be. He told them. They expected it to be less but said that one way or the other they would raise the money, and they subsequently did.

A few days before Russell was to appear, his hosts called and told him that before his talk the faculty was giving a luncheon in his honor. He was of course asked to attend. Russell said he would, but that doing so would require payment of an additional fee.

MORAL: There's no such thing as a free lunch.

The more productive people are and the more important their work, the more others expect free access to their time. That people want access to their time is not surprising; that they expect it is. The time of others is too often thought of as a free commodity rather than as their most valued resource. For productive people, time is always in short supply and nonrenewable. Requests for time that are reasonable when considered separately often amount to more time than the recipient has available when added together. Yet I have found nothing that angers people as much as a denial of a request for time, and their anger is usually inversely proportional to the value they place on their own time.

Attitudes toward time are not only matters of personality, but also of culture, as we will see in the next chapter.

Chapter Six

Ask for Anything You Like Except Time

Culture, Language, and Customs

❦ ❦ ❦

People count up the faults of those who keep them waiting.

—French proverb

Those who make the worst use of their time are the first to complain of its brevity.

—Jean de la Bruyere

❦ ❦ ❦   *Mexican Congestion*

One day during my sabbatical year in Mexico I received a call from a friend who was one of Mexico City's planners. He asked for a meeting because he thought I might be able to help with a problem he had. We arranged to get together in my office. He appeared as planned, heavily armed with charts and maps.

After we exchanged the usual greetings, he told me that the mayor of Mexico City had asked him to prepare a transportation plan for that city that would significantly reduce the congestion and travel time experienced by its residents. My friend had developed six alternative plans, and he proceeded to show me each. One focused on enlarging the subway system, another on widening streets, yet another on the bus system, and so on. When he had shown me all the plans, he said the mayor expected a single recommendation, not a set of alternatives. How, my friend asked, could he determine which of the six plans was the best?

Apologizing in advance for what I was about to say, I told him I didn't think any of the plans would solve the problem they addressed. Nat-

urally, he was taken aback by my statement. He asked for an explanation, which I gave.

I pointed out that, using conventional origin-destination studies, he had estimated the amount of unsatisfied demand for transportation in the city. Then he had prepared plans in which the supply of transportation was increased enough to handle the amount of unfilled demand that he had estimated. However, I continued, he had failed to consider the increase in demand for transportation that would be produced by the increases in supply he proposed. I cited the experience of other cities in which it was learned that the increased amount of demand generated by increased supply often exceeded the amount of demand satisfied by the increased supply. Therefore, increasing the supply of transportation often increases congestion and travel time.

"If you can't reduce congestion and travel time by increasing supply," *he asked, "how can you reduce it?"*

I answered, "By decreasing demand."

He said this could not be done in a democracy.

"Not true," I said. "There are a number of ways it can be done without violating democratic principles."

"Name one," he said.

I suggested moving all or part of the capital of Mexico out of Mexico City. I pointed out that significantly more than half the people employed in the city were either directly or indirectly employed by the federal government. Not only would moving the capital of Mexico out of Mexico City reduce the population, and therefore congestion and travel time, more than all of his plans put together, but it would have very desirable economic and social consequences: dispersing the capital would spread development more evenly over the country. (At that time Mexico City was receiving several times as much investment-per-capita in improvement as any other Mexican city.)

My friend objected. "You can't move a nation's capital."

"Yes you can," I replied. "The United States did it twice."

"Yes, but that was about two hundred years ago," he countered.

"Then what about Brazil?" I asked.

"Even that was a couple of decades ago," he said.

"Then how about Tanzania, which is planning to move its capital right now?"

"Come on," he said. "You can't compare Mexico to an African nation. You don't seem to understand that Mexico City was capital of the Aztec empire."

"I know that," I said. "But what has that got to do with it?"

"You will never understand," he said, "because you are not a Mexican. Believe me, given the Mexican culture, the capital cannot be moved."

There seemed to be no point to further argument, so the two of us sat there silently for a few minutes. Then he asked, "Do you have any other crazy ideas?"

I said I did. He asked for one.

"Change the working hours," I said. "Many people working in this city take a three-hour lunch break in the middle of the day. This is still called the siesta, even though it is seldom used for sleeping. Because the break is so long, many go home for lunch. This produces a great deal more traffic than would a shorter lunch hour, such as we have in the United States. Furthermore, it would give working parents much more time with their children in the evenings."

Again, my friend told me that changing the siesta was not possible; it was too deeply ingrained in the Mexican culture. When I pointed out that cultures change even in fundamental ways, he said this was not so for Mexico. I pointed out the tremendous change from the Indian-dominated to the Spanish-dominated culture of Mexico. He said this change had been imposed on Mexico from without; it was not a voluntary change and, therefore, was not relevant. Once again he referred to the fact that I was not a Mexican and, therefore, probably would not understand this. Another awkward silence followed.

After several more tries on my part, we both gave up. He did not consider any of my suggestions to be feasible; each was rejected for cultural reasons.

A few months later José Lopez Portillo was inaugurated as president of Mexico. In his inaugural address he announced his intention of moving at least part of the capital out of Mexico City and of changing working hours in the city by reducing the length of the siesta.

Where was the impossibility of these changes that my friend, the planner, had seen? Not in the Mexican culture, but in his mind.

> **MORAL: The principal obstruction between man
> and what he desires most is man himself.**

Mexico

As I have said, I spent the academic year 1975–76 at the National Autonomous University of Mexico (UNAM) in Mexico City. Most of that time was spent on research projects carried out for a variety of government agencies. However, I taught one graduate class in the College of Engineering. It was there that I had my first lesson on the subject of Mexican time.

❦ ❦ ❦   ***Time on My Hands***

My class was scheduled for late Monday afternoons. I arrived at the designated classroom for the first session of my class a few minutes before its scheduled starting time. No one was there. I thought I might be in the wrong room so I returned to the departmental office to check it. I had not made a mistake, but the departmental secretary told me that classes in Mexico normally start from 30 to 45 minutes after their scheduled starting time. Neither professors nor students usually appear before then.

I returned to the assigned classroom, which was still empty, and waited for the students. They began to arrive about a half-hour late. I said nothing, but began the class when a quorum had gathered, about 45 minutes late.

On the following week, I again appeared at the classroom on time. This time I began lecturing to an absolutely empty room. When the first student arrived about 15 minutes later, he could not understand my behavior. However, he took a seat and began to take notes on the lecture I was giving. Others arrived later and took their seats while I continued without commenting on their lateness.

On the third week, when I began to lecture at the scheduled time, the room was virtually full.

MORAL: To be free is to control one's own time;
it can be given to, but never should be
taken by, another.

The Mexican attitude toward time turned out to be a great deal more flexible than I suspected. This was reflected in one of the research projects on which I was engaged. A team consisting of five Mexicans and myself carried out a project for CONASUPO, the Mexican basic commodity agency. We met two to three times each week, and each time we met the meeting did not begin for at least a half hour after its scheduled starting time because of late arrivals. I suggested this was not fair to those who arrived on time and, therefore, that latecomers should be required to pay one peso for each minute they were late. (A peso still had some value at that time.) This money was to go into a pool that would pay for a party when the project was completed. The suggestion was accepted. From then on team members were seldom late and, when they were, they were seldom more than a few minutes late. Although we did not raise enough money through fines to pay for a party at the end of the project, we had one anyhow.

I was not nearly as successful in dealing with a high-ranking official of the Ministry of National Patrimony.

❧ ❧ ❧   *A Wait-Reduction Program*

The project in the Ministry of National Patrimony on which I worked required frequent meetings with the responsible director general. At his insistence, these meetings were always held in his office and were scheduled at his convenience. Nevertheless, I was repeatedly kept waiting for more than half an hour each time I appeared for a meeting. I was particularly annoyed because it was usually quite apparent that no one had been in his office while I was kept waiting. After several such occasions I complained to him. He apologized and assured me it would not happen again.

It did; on my next visit I was kept waiting for more than 45 minutes. When I entered his office, he told me he had been kept on the phone by a very important call. I tried to explain to him that I could not spend a significant part of the limited time I had in Mexico waiting for him. Therefore, the next time I came for a meeting with him, I would wait for no more than 10 minutes. If the meeting did not start within that interval, I would leave. He assured me it would not be necessary, but it was.

On my next visit, after I had been waiting about five minutes his deputy appeared, sat down at my side, and began to chat with me. I told him I suspected he had been sent out to keep me there beyond the threatened 10-minute limit, but despite this I would be leaving in a minute or two if I had not been called by then. He pleaded with me to wait a bit longer, but I refused. When the 10 minutes were up, I rose and walked to the elevator. Before an elevator arrived, the official who had kept me waiting came running down the hall and asked me to see him then. I refused, and told him that if he wanted to see me again he would have to come to my office at a time convenient to me. I assured him that if he came, he would not have to wait.

The director general was offended by my behavior. As a result, he terminated the contract he administered. When another contract with a different part of the same ministry was given to us the next day, the official responsible for the new project was well aware of what had happened to the previous project. He was delighted, he told me in confidence, because he disliked intensely the official I had offended.

> **MORAL: Time is our most valuable resource, the only one that is absolutely nonrenewable. No one, including us, has the right to waste it.**

Some to whom I've told these time-related stories think I was wrong to try to make Mexicans comply with an American's attitude toward time rather than to accommodate to theirs. I disagree because I believe the Mexican attitude toward time is one of the principal reasons for their slow development.

In Mexico, time is allocated to work using a priority system that is based on the rank of the one who asks for the time. This raises havoc with schedules and appointments. Anyone can be bumped from a schedule because someone higher subsequently wants that time. Appointments are often cancelled at the last minute or simply not kept. It is very difficult, often impossible, to make effective use of time made available at the last moment.

Lateness is the rule in Mexico; waiting is a national pastime. It is accepted with equanimity. Waiting rooms are plentiful; their size is directly proportional to the importance of the official whose waiting room it is.

President Luis Echeverría Alvarez, who held office while I was living in Mexico, was said to sleep only four hours per day and to work most of the rest of the time. This schedule had a significant ripple effect throughout the whole society. He expected the rest of the government to be on call whenever he was awake, and it was. For those on call, there was no regular workday. The same was true for those who worked for those who were on call, and so on down the hierarchy. One high-ranking government official told me that the inability to control one's own time was the principal reason for voluntary resignations from the government and the high incidence of divorce among those who remained.

The amount of time spent at work in Mexico is considered more important than the amount of work done, and the time of all one's inferiors or subordinates is treated as a free commodity. Although typical Mexicans work many more hours than typical Americans, they get considerably less work done because of their very poor use of time.

Despite my inclination to criticize Mexico for its attitude toward time, I am deeply in love with that country. I love it for its shortcomings as well as for its virtues. For example, I know of no other country in the world that has as wide a range of highly developed arts and crafts. Mexico's aesthetic sensibilities and creativity exceed ours by far. And I have never spent time in another country in which the natives were any warmer and friendlier. Whatever they may think of gringos in general did not seem to affect their attitudes toward me. As a result, I felt, and continue to feel, completely at home there.

Although the Mexicans appear to mess up most of their development efforts either through mismanagement or poor organization, they are capable of organized accomplishments that are amazing. For example, they planned for and were ready for the 1968 Olympics in less time than any other country has ever managed. Of course, the question remains as to why they waited so long to get started.

I participated in a project that began in September of one year and by February of the following year, in six months, we built the buildings for and started operation of a new campus of the National Autonomous University of Mexico capable of handling 30,000 students. Moreover, the academic design of this campus

was completely innovative, incorporating more unique sched-
uling, curricular, and pedagogical concepts than I have seen
anywhere else.

For example, the calendar year was broken into three equal
parts, trimesters. The undergraduate program was a three-year
program (see Figure 5). First-year students attended courses
their first two trimesters and worked in an organization outside
the university, but one relevant to their curriculum, in their
third trimester. In their second year they took courses in the
first and third trimester and worked in the second. In their
third year they worked in the first trimester and took courses
in the last two. This arrangement made it possible to reduce
physical requirements from those needed for 30,000 students
to those needed for 20,000, since one class was at work each
trimester. It also meant that the facilities provided were used
year-round and did not stay idle for several months each year,
as ours do. Moreover, each cooperating organization was provided with the number of students it requested for as long as
it wanted. As the students rotated in a particular organization,
the senior students who were leaving were responsible for ori-
enting and training the junior students coming in.

	Semester		
	First	Second	Third
First-year students	Class	Class	Work
Second-year students	Class	Work	Class
Third-year students	Work	Class	Class

❦ Figure 5

Literacy is highly valued in Mexico. I learned that many of the Mexicans who carry newspapers under their arms cannot read but like to give the impression that they can. In fact, some Americans who cannot read Spanish do the same, because it keeps street vendors and beggars from being a bother.

So many of the Mexicans I had to deal with professionally and socially spoke English so much better than I spoke Spanish that I never had an opportunity to improve my Spanish. One day I decided to do something about this lack of opportunity. I wrote out and practiced a good-morning speech to my secretary at the university. When I arrived she listened patiently as I stumbled through my greetings. When I had finished she meekly said in English, "Please, don't speak Spanish. It's hard enough to understand your English." That ended my effort to improve my Spanish.

Most college-educated Mexicans speak English well. Of those with advanced degrees, many were educated in the United States and tend to look north for intellectual leadership. Despite this, Mexican intellectuals are more committed to their country and culture than are intellectuals from most other countries. In almost a half century of teaching in advanced degree programs, I have had students from a very large number of countries, both more and less developed. Students from many of these are attracted by the greater opportunities for effective use of their knowledge in the United States than exist in their countries. They are also attracted by the higher standard of living and, in some cases, better quality of life. Students who come from some countries, especially India, try to stay in the States. However, this has hardly ever been the case with Mexicans. They go back to their country and stay there.

Mexicans do not merely like their country, they love it passionately. Their love is not directed at Mexico as a political entity, but rather Mexico as a culture. Mexicans are very proud of their culture and customs. They have a right to be, for they are works of art, literally as well as figuratively. The Mexican culture differs more from that of the United States than do the cultures of most European countries. Despite its proximity to the States, Mexico is more foreign than most European countries.

It is possible that Mexicans are too dedicated to their culture. As illustrated in the fable with which this chapter opened, they sometimes use it as an excuse for not doing things they should do, things that would accelerate their development.

India

My wife and I spent several months in India in 1957 as guests of its government. I had been invited there to critically evaluate its second five-year plan. The invitation had come from the chief architect of this plan, Professor P.C. Mahalanobis. He was one of Nehru's principal advisers. In addition to being India's chief national development planner, the professor was a world-famous statistician. He had made major contributions to the art and science of census taking. His Indian Statistical Institute was India's census bureau. Its primary location was in a large compound on the outskirts of Calcutta. He and his wife lived in the compound, which also contained several guest houses. My wife and I spent several weeks in one of them.

The three things that impressed me most about India were its aesthetics, its caste system, and its poverty. I was overwhelmed by the beauty of Indian architecture, painting, sculpture, music, dance, and crafts. The Indians seem capable of making anything into a thing of beauty. Even after having been exposed to a good deal of Indian architecture, I expected to be disappointed when I went to see the Taj Mahal. The widespread propaganda about its beauty made me skeptical—nothing could be that impressive. I was wrong; it was everything that was said about it and more. But the Taj was not alone; many other buildings were almost as impressive.

In contrast to their aesthetic treatment of things and their performing arts, their treatment of people, particularly those in the lowest caste, left a great deal to be desired. When staying in the homes of upper-caste Indians, we tried and often managed to communicate with the servants, and sometimes even with the untouchables who were employed to clean the lavatories. When caught doing this by our hosts, we were asked to stop because it created expectations in those with whom we spoke that would not subsequently be fulfilled. It was important, we were told, that the members of the lower castes be kept in their proper place.

I was surprised to learn that, as in the Western world up until the Renaissance, upper castes are reluctant to use their hands. Work with the hands is considered degrading and not proper for a person of status. I learned about this attitude toward the use of hands by putting my foot in my mouth.

❦ ❦ ❦   *Hand-me-downs*

I was having a discussion with a government official in his office in New Delhi when there was a knock on the door to the private entrance into his room. (Each office of an important person had both a public and a private entrance.) He called, "Come in." A distinguished-looking man entered and I was introduced to him. He was another high-ranking official. When he saw me he apologized for the interruption and then asked if he could borrow a particular book from my host. My host pulled the book off a shelf and handed it to the visitor. He examined it to make sure it was the one he wanted. It was. Then he placed it on the desk and said goodbye to my host and me. He began to leave the office without the book. I grabbed it and caught him before he reached the door, offering him the book I thought he'd forgot. He smiled condescendingly and continued out of the room, leaving me holding the book.

It was clear that I had done something wrong. I asked my host about it. He also smiled tolerantly and told me not to be concerned and to return the book to where it had been placed on his desk. I did so. A few minutes later there was another knock at the private entrance. Again my host called out, "Come in." This time it was obviously a servant of low caste, one frequently referred to in the States as a "gofer." He bowed deferentially, picked up the book, and left the room without saying a word.

Later, some Indian friends explained to me that it would have been improper for a man of the first visitor's importance and status to be seen carrying anything in public.

> **MORAL: The caste system is a way by which those who, because of an accident of birth, take privilege for granted and give a hard time to those who, because of an accident of birth, take it.**

Despite their disadvantaged condition and low position in society, there was no lack of shrewdness or cleverness among those in the lower castes. They were not well educated but they were far from stupid. They were neither as irrational as their critics alleged nor as irrational as their critics. This observation was related to the most important thing I learned in India: that rationality is relative.

As I noted earlier, it is commonplace for us to assume we understand the behavior of others. As a result, when they behave in a way that contradicts our expectations, we often attribute irrationality to them. Such rationalization of our incorrect expectations provides no understanding of the behavior of relevant others and prevents our being of greater service to them. (I learned this through an incident that I described in *The Art of Problem Solving* [1978]. I apologize for its repetition here to those who may have been exposed to it there. It illustrates the point too well to omit.)

❦ ❦ ❦   *An Immaculate Misconception*

While in India I met a number of Americans trying to peddle family planning and birth control to the natives. They were not succeeding. They blamed their failure on the irrationality of the Indians. Why couldn't the Indians understand that a rate of increase of their population that exceeds the rate of growth of their economy means decreasing income per capita?

The attribution of irrationality to the Indians left the Americans with no idea how to increase their effectiveness. After all, how can one cope with irrationality? When I suggested to one of the Americans at a party held at the Indian Statistical Institute that the Americans might be irrational and the Indians rational, he was shocked. He challenged me to give one good reason to consider seriously such a hypothesis. In response, I showed him a clipping I had taken from The New York Times *in which it was reported that a Brazilian woman had given birth to her forty-second child. I pointed out that the difference between 42 and the 4.6 children the average Indian family had was much larger than the difference between 4.6 and none. This suggested that the problem was not lack of control. The American said my line of argument was ridiculous and walked away.*

An Indian who had overheard this conversation came up to me and introduced himself. He was T.K. Balakrishnan, one of India's leading demographers. He apologized for eavesdropping but said he was fascinated by the possibility of demonstrating the rationality of India's population growth. He asked if I would be willing to work with him in an effort to do so. I said I would but that I would be leaving India shortly. However, I added quickly, I would be replaced by my colleague, Glen Camp, who would remain in India for some time. I was reasonably sure Glen would be willing to continue whatever Balakrishnan and I might get started.

We did get started and Camp did subsequently arrive and take it over. This is what Balakrishnan and Camp found: After obtaining its independence, India had increased the expected life span of adults dra-

matically, but it had not increased the span of employable life. Poor Indians, and most of them are, could expect to work for only the first half of their adult lives. Therefore, while young and employed, Indians had to try to arrange for financial security during the subsequent period in which they expected to be unemployed.

The Indian government provided no unemployment insurance or old-age security benefits. Very few Indians earned enough to insure themselves. Therefore, the only way most Indians could assure their survival during a long period of unemployment was by having enough employed children to provide the support required. On the average, one wage-earner could provide the minimal support required by one non-wage-earning adult. However, since only males were generally employable in India at that time, this implied a need for an average of four children, two boys and two girls, to support both father and mother. However, because of the high mortality rate among children born of poor Indians, the birth of slightly more than four was required to yield the four who would survive. The average family size in India corresponded almost exactly to this requirement.

The size of Indian families could, of course, have been due to other factors. However, Balakrishnan and Camp showed that it wasn't. If the security-based explanation of family size was correct, one would expect the family size of those couples whose first two or three children were sons to be smaller than those whose first few children were daughters. This was found to be the case.

Balakrishnan and Camp did not argue that old-age unemployment was the only factor affecting India's birth rate, but that it was critical. Therefore, to ask Indians to have fewer children was to ask them to commit a delayed suicide.

MORAL: Irrationality is more likely to be found in the mind of the beholder than in the mind of the beheld.

India's poverty was more pervasive and more severe than I have seen anywhere before or since. The streets and public places were filled with the homeless. Thousands slept at night on sidewalks and on the floor of the central railroad station in Calcutta. To see them was depressing and frustrating because there was nothing an individual visitor could do to alleviate their suffering. If one made the mistake of giving something to one of the ever-present beggars, one would immediately be surrounded by others who wanted the same. My wife and I frequently had to be rescued from such sieges by Indian friends.

Despite this we found that even the poorest Indians were unbelievably generous. Our experience with Kirpal Singh was only one of many examples of this.

❦ ❦ ❦   *Kirpal Singh*

During part of my stay in India I was scheduled to work with Pitambar Panth, head of the government's planning staff, in New Delhi. My wife and I were scheduled to be his house guests during our stay there. Unfortunately, his young daughter came down with the measles just before we were to arrive. His house was quarantined. Therefore, we were put up in a first-class hotel.

In the weeks prior to our trip to New Delhi I had fallen in love with Indian music, so much so that my wife decided to surprise me by buying an Indian instrument for my use. One day, while I was at work with the planning staff, she asked at the desk of the hotel where she might buy a set of used tablas, Indian drums. She was given instructions that she gave to a taxi driver outside the hotel. The driver took her to the store. She asked him to wait while she did her shopping. She returned later to the waiting cab with the tablas she had bought.

The driver of the taxi, a young Sikh named Kirpal Singh, knew only a few words of English, but he managed to let my wife know that he played tablas. When she made it clear that the tablas were for me but that I did not know how to play them, he volunteered to come to our hotel that evening and give me instruction. My wife accepted his generous offer.

That evening Kirpal appeared and we had a wonderful time. I had my harmonica with me. I played American music for him, and he Indian music for me. In between he instructed me on use of the tablas. I had room service bring dinner for the three of us to our room, where we made a full night of it. (Shortly after dinner was brought to our room, the hotel manager appeared to make sure we were not being bothered by our visiting Sikh. When we assured him all was well, he left reluctantly.)

The next day, when my wife left the hotel to begin her explorations, Kirpal was waiting with his cab at the hotel's entrance and insisted she come with him. He took her on a tour of the city and insisted on buying her lunch. He would not accept payment even for his taxi. He did the same every day of that week, including the weekend, when I had some free time. We continued to spend our evenings together as well, doing violence to instruments, music, and the hotel manager's opinion of us.

We learned from Kirpal that he had been married and had had several children. At that time he had lived in East Bengal. He lost his family during the uprising in the latter part of the 1950s. He and a brother had managed to escape and migrate to New Delhi.

Like all good things, our relationship with Kirpal had to come to an end. He knew which day we were to leave for the States. Early on the morning of our departure he and a friend who could speak a little English appeared at our hotel room with flowers for my wife. Through him Kirpal told us he was concerned lest we did not have enough money to get back home. He offered to help us if we needed it. I don't know how he got the idea that we might be short of funds, but his generosity in offering to help us was overwhelming. We assured him we had enough funds to get home.

Then we exchanged gifts. While doing so, my official host, Pitambar Panth, appeared with a limousine to drive us to the airport. Kirpal would not hear of it. He insisted that he take us there. We finally compromised. He took my wife; I went in the government's limousine. We met at the airport, where we had a very tearful farewell.

> **MORAL:** *The art of giving is much less developed*
> *than the art of receiving, but it is more developed*
> *among the less developed than among the*
> *more developed.*

It is my impression that the poor in less-developed nations are among the most generous people in the world, much more generous than the wealthy in well-developed nations.

I find it very difficult, if not impossible, to return to India despite its beauty and charm. The dominant memory I have of it is of being completely surrounded by abject poverty about which I could do nothing and to which the affluent Indians have become inured. It made me feel physically ill much of the time. I am aware, of course, that my not seeing something does not make it go away, but if I must see something I cannot tolerate, I prefer it to be something I can do something about.

My reaction to poverty in other less developed countries has not been nearly as strong, perhaps because the poverty has not been as pervasive or as abject in any of the others. In India one senses that those living in poverty have little if any chance of improving their lot. In no other country have I sensed such absolute hopelessness, but Mexico came close.

Holland

Language is also a frequent obstruction to getting what one wants.

❦ ❦ ❦   *Bringing Up Bottoms*

My wife, three children, and I drove south from Denmark to Bilthoven, a town south of Amsterdam, in Holland. Our youngest, my daughter Karla, was still in diapers. In Denmark we had come upon a good disposable diaper that went under the brand name Sanex. Therefore, whenever we wanted replacements in Denmark, we simply asked for the diapers by their brand name and the storekeepers brought us what we wanted.

As we approached Amsterdam my wife said we had better stop and replenish our supply of diapers. When I saw a Dutch version of our drug store, I stopped and we went in. A man who looked like the owner came to serve us. We asked for Sanex. He nodded, went into the back room and reappeared with a small unlabeled package wrapped in brown paper. The package was obviously too small to contain diapers. With gestures we indicated that we wanted something bigger. He nodded and disappeared again. He reappeared shortly with another small package, but larger than the first, similarly wrapped. Once again we indicated that what we wanted was larger. He nodded, but with a surprised look on his face, and disappeared again. He returned with another small but larger package, similarly wrapped. Again we indicated that we needed something larger. At this point he expressed disbelief by gesture and words we did not understand, but he made it clear to us that there was nothing bigger.

My wife and I decided that whatever he was bringing us, it was not diapers. Therefore, I drew a handkerchief from my pocket, put it on the counter and folded it slowly like a diaper. The attendant exclaimed, indicating that he finally understood. With a look of great relief he disappeared again, this time reappearing with a package of the diapers we wanted.

We then learned that Sanex was also the brand name of sanitary napkins.

> **MORAL: Words may conceal as well as reveal meaning.**

England

The same word can mean different things in different countries. I learned this in England. I wanted to buy some wood slats to repair the coal bin in the house provided by the University of Birmingham at which I was a visiting professor for the academic year. I asked a neighboring shopkeeper where I could find a lumberyard. He looked at me with surprise and said he did not know. I was surprised. I tried another storekeeper and got the same response. When I tried for a third time, the storekeeper asked what I wanted from a lumberyard. I told him. He then informed me that what we wanted was a timber yard, and he told me where I could find one. When I asked him what a lumberyard was, we learned that "lumber" means "trash" in England. A lumberyard is a dump there.

Most people who have visited the U.K. learn that a lorry is a truck, a lift is an elevator, that chips are french fries, and so on and on. No wonder Oscar Wilde once wrote that England and the United States were two countries separated only by a common language.

Perhaps the greatest difficulty with language arises between two people whose primary tongue is the same, because what is said and what is heard are often very different things. I once heard a story that illustrates this point perfectly.

❦ ❦ ❦   *Goddamned Cereal*

A young married couple had twins as their first progeny, a boy and a girl. The children survived infancy and eventually entered kindergarten. Shortly after they had, the principal of their school called their mother and asked her to come to his office. There was a problem involving her children. He assured her, however, that they had suffered no bodily harm. It was not that kind of a problem.

The mother hurriedly dressed and drove to the school, where she was immediately shown into the principal's office. He was obviously embarrassed and had difficulty getting to the point. The mother, now almost frantic, insisted that he tell her what was wrong.

He braced himself and asked, "Do you realize that your children use an inordinate amount of profanity and obscenity in their speech?"

After a pause, she said, "Yes. Their father is a traveling salesman and he talks that way around the house. The children have picked it up from him, but you don't have to worry; they don't understand what the words mean."

"I do have to worry," the principal responded. "Other children are picking up the bad words and taking them home. Their parents are complaining and threatening to remove their children from this school. I have no choice: unless you can clean up your children's speech quickly, I am going to have to expel them."

The mother was greatly upset but assured the principal that she and her husband would take care of the problem one way or another. She returned home and resumed her normal routine until late that night, when the children were in bed and her husband returned from a trip. He no sooner entered the house than she put the problem to him. He acknowledged his responsibility for it and, after some discussion, suggested that his wife stay in bed the next morning while he went down, prepared breakfast for the children, and had a heart-to-heart talk with them. She agreed.

The next morning he was in the kitchen getting things ready when the two children entered, the son first. The father asked him what he would like for breakfast.

He said, "I'd like some of those goddamned corn flakes." The father slapped the boy hard across his face and sent him spinning across the room. Before the boy even began to cry, the father turned to the daughter and asked her what she wanted for breakfast.

She replied, "You can be goddamned sure I don't want any of those goddamned corn flakes."

MORAL: More than words of wisdom come out of the mouths of babes.

I've had a love affair with England for a very long time. I have found its intellectual environment the least inhibited and the most stimulating in the world. It is not a particularly good place to implement change, but it is undoubtedly the best place to think and talk about it. For example, the freedom of speech exercised in Hyde Park on a Sunday morning or in the letters to the editor of English newspapers is unparalleled in the United States. This freedom extends to all the broadcast media.

My family and I arrived for our year in England in the summer of 1959. One of the first things we did after we settled into the living quarters was to go out and rent a television set. That set was delivered to us late that (Saturday) night. We turned it on early on Sunday morning and obtained BBC's weekly religious broadcast. It consisted of a debate between the Archbishop of Canterbury and a prominent female intellectual on religion versus atheism. There are many atheists in the United States, of course, but few would dare to express themselves to this effect in public, particularly on television, even if the networks would permit it, and they wouldn't; atheism is not a legitimate belief, or lack of belief, in the United States. It is in England, and is only one of a large set of beliefs that must be concealed in our country but is discussed over there openly and without shame.

Curiously, during World War II, I was told, those who on induction to the military indicated they had no religion were registered as members of the Church of England. That's one way to keep the membership up.

England loves eccentrics of every type, particularly intellectual eccentrics. It is not accidental that the three men who have probably had the most radical effects on contemporary thought—Darwin, Marx, and Freud—all did their major work in England. England produces and nurtures new ideas as no other country does. It has not nurtured art in the same way, except in literature. England's principal contribution to aesthetics lies in the use of words; literature has been its forte, and its actors have been and are superb. I have never seen bad acting in England and very seldom seen bad plays, even when I've selected the ones to see at random.

I have never had a bad time in England, but I have had some surprising ones.

❦ ❦ ❦   *Back Talk*

On my first visit to England I was asked to deliver a lecture to the Operational Research Society of the United Kingdom. The lecture took place one evening in London in a large auditorium. After I made my presentation, Dr. K.D. Tocher, who shared the stage with the chairman and me, rose and said to me before the audience that I was probably not familiar with the English custom of having someone assigned to criticize a paper after its presentation. He said that he had been asked to do so and hoped I would not be offended. I was surprised by this but said I would not be offended.

"Toch," as he was called, proceeded to tear my paper apart. When he was finished, I arose and explained to him and the audience that in the United States, when a public presentation was attacked publicly, we retaliated in kind. I then proceeded to tear his criticism of my paper apart. A very lively discussion followed and a great time was had by all.

**MORAL: Talking back can sometimes move
things forward.**

That evening made friends of Toch and me. Among other things, he helped me become aware of a significant difference between England and the United States. In the United States one does not ordinarily attack a public presentation made by a friend; in England one attacks only those public presentations made by friends. This reflects the detachment with which the English can deal with ideas, and our lack of ability to do so. In the United States, agreement and affection are highly and positively correlated; not so in England. I like to like people I don't agree with and to dislike some of those with whom I agree. This removes restrictions from both the heart and the mind; it gives them a larger arena in which to exercise.

France

I am ashamed to admit that I am not a Francophile. My bias against France derives from several linguistic experiences I had there. These have dominated all the exciting aesthetic experiences France has afforded me. Late-nineteenth-century French painting and the French Gothic cathedral seem to me to have come close to perfection. Nevertheless, my experiences with the French language override my feelings about the country's artistic accomplishments. The French are fussier about their language than any other people whose country I have visited. They are the only ones who have repeatedly made me feel uncomfortable, if not unwelcome, because I do not speak their language fluently.

🐛 🐛 🐛   *On Franglish*

In the early 1970s I was invited to Paris for a roundtable discussion of national energy problems. The meeting was hosted by a ministry of the French government. About 20 people had been invited, including several from the United States. The meetings were held in a beautiful chateau near Versailles.

We gathered at the designated time and place and were greeted by a deputy minister who was to serve as chairman of the meeting. He addressed us in English and asked, "Is there anyone here who is not conversant in French?"

One other attendee and I raised our hands.

"Well," he said, "since there are only two of you, we will conduct the meetings in French." And he proceeded to do so.

I left shortly thereafter.

❦ ❦ ❦

Several years later, the university-based research group of which I was a part contracted for a planning project that dealt with the city of Paris. The project was conducted for a committee of the French cabinet. The French were apparently ashamed to use an American group. Therefore, they contracted for the work with a government agency, which subcontracted it with a French consulting firm that, in turn, subsubcontracted it with us.

Our contract contained several unusual requirements: All students employed by us to work on the project had to be French citizens, and all faculty members who went to France on project work had to be conversant in French. In addition, the final report of the work had to be written in French.

The fact is that all the work done on the project both here and in France was done in English, but every effort was made to make it appear to have been done in France in French.

❦ ❦ ❦

Again, several years later, I attended an international conference held in Aix-en-Provence in southern France. The conferees came from many countries, but considerably more of them could speak English than any other language. Few could speak French. However, the opening address delivered to the conference was made in French by a very distinguished French social scientist. His presentation was translated sequentially by one of his graduate students: He delivered a paragraph in French; his student then translated the paragraph. He followed with another paragraph, and so on. This staccato presentation was very annoying to most of the audience and spoiled what was otherwise an excellent lecture.

Questions were invited at the end of the presentation. Almost all of them were formulated in English. The presenter's student translated them into French. The speaker then replied in French and was translated back into English by the student.

One particularly complicated but important question was asked in English. The answer, given in French, was equally complicated. Half-way through the student's translation of it, the speaker broke in and said in almost perfect English that the student was translating his reply incorrectly. He completed the translation himself. Once done, he reverted to French.

**MORAL: Even a beautiful language can be spoken
by an ugly person.**

Russia

When I first visited the Soviet Union I experienced something I had previously experienced only once, in Japan: complete disorientation. I could not read any of the signs. We tend to forget that we can read signs in languages other than our own if they use the Latin alphabet. But if they do not, we can't read street signs or signs on buildings. This makes it extremely difficult to find one's way around.

To make things worse, not only do the Russians use a different alphabet from ours, but they use a different word order.

✼ ✼ ✼   The U.S.S.R.

A validated hotel reservation was required for admission to Russia. I had been told that a reservation had been made for me by my hosts at the Soviet Academy of Sciences. However, after customs and immigration, when I went through the hotel-reservation filter at the airport, the young lady in charge could not find my name on her list of approved entrants. I explained my situation to her and even showed her the letter that named the hotel at which a reservation had been made for me. She consulted her list again and assured me I was not on it. Despite my protests, she called a guard and I was escorted to a small, unoccupied room and told to sit down until a return flight could be arranged for me. I was then left alone.

Fortunately, and unbeknownst to me, a small deputation from the academy had come to meet me at the airport. When I failed to appear they made a number of inquiries and eventually learned of my disposition. By pulling rank, they managed to get to the room I occupied and called for the young lady and the list that had led to my banishment. When she appeared, they asked her to consult her list again because, they assured her, a hotel reservation had been made for me. While she was reexamining her list, a possible source of the error occurred to me. I suggested she look for Ackoff Russell. She found it immediately. Apologies were given and I was permitted to enter Russia.

For the next two weeks I had to identify myself as Ackoff Russell to all Russian institutions and agencies. After all, this was the way my name was printed in my passport.

> **MORAL: It is better to walk backward to where
> one wants to go than to walk forward to where
> one doesn't.**

There was another aspect of Russian life that I failed to learn about from reading.

ぎ ぎ ぎ　　　　　*Out of Space*

I have a Russian friend, Igor Ushakov, who, on his first visit to the United States, spent several days as a guest in my home. At that time my family and I lived in a large, old, three-story Dutch colonial house in a Philadelphia suburb. Igor had a bedroom and a bath to himself during his stay. Each weekday he went to the university with me, where he lectured and conducted several seminars. In the evenings and on the weekend we did a little sight-seeing, some socializing, and a lot of shopping.

One evening, Igor and I went to a spirited and friendly social gathering of university people. It went into the early hours of the morning. When we returned to my house, I asked Igor if he would like something to drink before he retired. He said he would very much like some hot tea. I made some and joined him.

Over the tea, Igor told me how much he appreciated the opportunity to experience the American way of life from the inside out. In turn, I told him how much I valued getting to know a Russian scientist as a friend, one with whom I could talk freely. He then asked if he could put some questions to me that he had always wanted to ask an American but had never before felt he could do comfortably. I said I would try to answer any question he asked, but would like to reciprocate with my own questions addressed to him. He agreed and we started. The conversation lasted until sunrise.

At one point I asked Igor, "If you could take back to Russia any aspect of the American way of life that you have seen, what would you take?"

He answered without hesitation, "Space."

I said I did not understand. He explained, "Space, living room. I was never in a house this big. My family and I live in an apartment that is very small by your standards, but very large by ours. Our place is so small that none of us can ever have any privacy at home."

This explanation surprised me, but I did not really appreciate it until I visited Igor's apartment in Moscow a year or so later. His apartment consisted of three rooms and a bath. The largest room was about 10-by-12 feet and served as living room, dining room, and master bedroom. Whenever its function was changed, furniture had to be moved about. His mother-in-law and children slept in the one very small bedroom. The kitchen could barely hold two persons at a time.

This apartment was considered luxurious by most Russians. Few had this much living room.

Because there was virtually no chance for most Russians to get any privacy at home, and because so few owned automobiles, I could not help but ask where teenagers did their necking in the winter. My question evoked a lot of laughter but little illumination.

❦ ❦ ❦

The scarcity of space was not restricted to living quarters. One day I called on the Russian publisher who had printed translations of several *of my books and articles. I entered a very large working area that was crowded with desks. Each one was occupied and had at least one person standing beside it, usually talking to the one seated. I asked who all those standing by the desks were. I was told that there were not enough desks for everyone, so several people alternated using each desk. Those standing were waiting for their turn and, as far as I could tell, were keeping those using the desks from getting much work done.*

MORAL: Every member of the public has a right to privacy.

We in the United States take living room and work space for granted. They should be treated as necessities, not luxuries. They may not be sufficient for democracy, but without them democracy is very difficult to realize. Space and privacy make for more autonomous individuals and a society that is seen as serving its members rather than as being served by them. Those who seldom if ever enjoy privacy develop a herd-like mentality, a capacity for *followership*. Wills cannot be free unless they have space to move around in. This is why rugged individualism is so strongly associated with those who live in the wide-open spaces.

Space is not the only thing in short supply in Russia. Few consumer goods are plentiful, especially clothing.

❧ ❧ ❧   *The Wash-and-Wear-and-Wash Cycle*

On my first trip to Russia, Igor Ushakov was among those who met me on my arrival at the Moscow Airport. He took me to the hotel at which a room had been reserved for me. I asked him to come with me to my room while I unpacked. I told him it would take only a few minutes and then I would be free to leave with him. He came along. As I unpacked, he watched with great interest. Although I had come for a two-week visit, I brought only three changes of clothing in addition to what I was wearing. Most of it was of the wash-and-wear type.

Igor asked me if I had brought all my clothing with me or had I left some of it at home. The question surprised me. I told him I had brought only a small portion of the clothing I owned. He then asked me how many shirts, pairs of socks, shoes, suits, and so on I had all together. I stopped in the middle of this inquisition to ask him why he was so interested in the size of my wardrobe. He replied that what he had seen me unpack together with what I was wearing was almost exactly equivalent to his entire wardrobe.

This exchange made me realize how excessive my wardrobe was, and how meager his was. When I asked him how he managed with so few clothes, he said his wife had to wash clothes every night, and she did not have access to automatic washing and drying equipment.

Later, when I met Igor's wife, we talked at length about the relative conditions of women in the United States and Russia. She told me that Russian women had been liberated by their revolution, long before American women. She went on to explain: She was free to hold any full-time job for which she was qualified. At the end of the work day she was free to spend the two hours or more required each day for shopping. Then she was free to prepare the evening meal and clean up afterward. She could then spend some time with her children, often helping them with their homework. After they went to bed she was free to do the laundry. We did not discuss what she was free to do after that.

> **MORAL: One is free to do something only if one controls the consequences of not doing it.**

Japan

My first visit to Japan occurred as a member of the U.S. Army of occupation in 1945. Although I have been back there a number of times since, the major memories I have of that country are rooted in my first exposure to it. Working in the engineering section of 8th Army's headquarters, I participated in planning that occupation. Just before we embarked from the Philippines for Japan, an order was issued to all troops taking part in the occupation to the effect that when we landed in Japan we were to drive on the right as we did at home, not on the left as the Japanese did. After all, who won the war?

I wrote a memo to the office that issued the order to the effect that driving on the right would cause havoc in Japan. Streetcars were running the other way with their unloading platforms placed accordingly, and signal lights for automobiles and pedestrians were located for driving on the left. My concern was summarily dismissed.

When we landed in Japan and began driving on the right, pandemonium followed. The Japanese continued to drive on the left. The army was forced to rescind the order to drive on the right almost immediately.

A culture can be changed, but seldom easily. Sweden, it will be recalled, did shift from left-hand to right-hand driving early in the 1960s, but only after making elaborate plans over an extended period of time and carrying out an extensive educational program. Even so, the Swedish shift was regarded by many as a kind of miracle.

We may have won the war, but the cultural changes required of the army of occupation in Japan were much greater than those required of the Japanese.

❦ ❦ ❦   *Washing Out the War*

An old silk mill had been selected for the headquarters of the 8th Army in Japan. It was one of the few buildings in Yokohama that had not been seriously damaged. When we moved into that building we found a room with parallel perforated pipes running along its ceiling. The room had obviously once been used to wet down silk. A decision was rapidly made to fix the room so that it could be used for showers. A team of engineers was put on it that first day. The next morning, when we went down to that room to take showers, we found it completely occupied and in use by the young ladies who had been hired to clean our building. They giggled when they saw us, but showed no signs of embarrassment. The reactions of these young ladies and of the American soldiers were not symmetrical.

MORAL: Cleanliness can have other effects than holiness.

We were later to learn that Japanese culture differed from ours in a major respect. In our culture we do in private what we all do in common—for example, bathe and eliminate waste. But we do in public many things that are unique to a specific individual—for example, kiss, hug, or embrace a particular person of the opposite sex. In Japan this was reversed: Members of the opposite sex bathed together and used the same lavatories at the same time, but one seldom if ever saw a man embrace, kiss, or even touch a woman in public. Most of us came to think that the Japanese customs were more rational than ours.

The young ladies who worked for the army of occupation, like most Japanese, were very anxious to please. Those who were employed to operate the elevators in the Daichi Building in Tokyo, where the headquarters of the army of occupation were established, asked some of the soldiers stationed there to teach them how to say "good morning" in English. They were instructed, all right. A few days after we landed in Japan, when I went to that building on business and entered one of its elevators, a pretty young lady in uniform bowed deeply and, with a big smile on her face, quite clearly said, "Oh, my aching back." All the Americans on the elevator with me smiled back and repeated the greeting. I often wondered how long it took those young ladies to realize the awful truth.

The Japanese seemed to be as happy over the ending of the war as we were. When we landed at Yokohama they lined the docks waving American flags. In the days and weeks that followed, I never sensed hate or resentment on their part, but I often sensed gratitude.

❧ ❧ ❧   *On Driving Drunks Back Home*

Another soldier and I were sent north to Hokkaido on a military mission. We were the first of the army of occupation to take a train north from Tokyo the length of Japan's main island, Honshu. Half of a railroad car was roped off for our exclusive use. The remainder of our car filled up quickly; many had to stand in the aisles. We removed the rope and allowed the Japanese to move into "our" half of the car. They were very grateful.

About half way up the island we took on a large contingent of soldiers who had just been separated from the Japanese army. Many of them were drunk. They entered our car at the far end and proceeded down the aisle, rudely pushing aside the closely packed Japanese, many of them older people. My colleague and I saw the fuss approaching us. (We could see them because of our height, but they could not see us.) We rose and stood in the aisle in the path of the oncoming soldiers. When they broke through and saw us standing there, fully armed, they fell to the floor prostrate. Fear seemed to sober them instantaneously. We told them to get up and go back through the car, undoing all the disruption they had wrought, and then leave the car. When they did, the Japanese in our car applauded loudly and began to shower us with gifts. I don't think I have ever been pampered as much as I was on the remainder of that trip.

MORAL: Giving others a hand often attracts a hand in return.

Like the Mexicans, the Japanese have a wonderful sense of beauty, an ability to bestow it on almost anything. But their beauty is very different from that created by the Mexicans.

Their beauty is precise, sharp, and very compact, whereas that of the Mexicans is rough, robust, and expansive. They seem to fall at opposite ends of the scale. The bonzai tree exemplifies the Japanese concept of beauty; the Mayan temple that of the Mexicans.

The Japanese, of course, have a lot more worth imitating than their sense of beauty. Their post-war "miracle" has most of the world in awe, and with justification. They have effectively used much more of what the Western world knows than the Western world has used. There is still a great deal that we in the West know that neither they in the East nor we have used, but they are more likely to use it in time than we. The Japanese take the long view and embrace change; we do neither. Our self-satisfaction has condemned us to a continuous and increasing maladaptation to our changing environment.

We used to think the Japanese got to where they are by imitating us. Not true; they got there by doing better than we, and it is we who are trying to imitate them. One cannot catch up to another by imitating him; one has to leap over him. The Japanese did this to us. At this time, it does not seem likely that we will do the same to them.

United States

It is very difficult, if at all possible, to place oneself outside one's own culture so that one can see it as others do. Nevertheless, I have observed a number of peculiarities of our culture over the years.

Among the characteristics that seem to me to be almost exclusively ours is an overabundance of righteous indignation. Once morality sets into an issue in the United States, there seems to be no way of dealing with it rationally. For example, one only has to consider the attitude toward smoking that has developed in the United States. Smoking has come to be considered much more than harmful to one's health; it is considered immoral.

❦ ❦ ❦   *Smoking, Cancer, and Cholera*

One of the first studies to associate smoking and cancer consisted of a correlation between per-capita consumption of tobacco and per-capita incidence of lung cancer. It was reported in a very reputable medical journal and was based on data collected from 21 countries. Although one cannot legitimately infer causal relationships from correlations, the authors indicated that it would be prudent to assume such a relationship and desist from smoking.

As one who knows a little about statistical inference, I was outraged by the logic employed by the authors. I could not deny that there might be a causal connection between lung cancer and smoking, but I could deny that the study provided any evidence that this was the case. (I was a heavy pipe smoker at the time.) My problem was how to make this point as powerfully as I could.

Using the reported data on smoking from the same countries and data that I obtained on the per-capita incidence of cholera in these countries, I, too, carried out a correlation analysis. I found a negative correlation that was stronger than the positive correlation that the authors of the lung cancer study had found. Then, using the same logic as they had used, I drew the conclusion that it would be prudent to smoke in order to prevent cholera.

I wrote this up using the same words as were in the article on cancer, changing as few as possible, and submitted the result to the same medical journal as had published the original article. My article was rejected and returned to me, but with no explanation. I wrote the editor, saying I thought I was entitled to an explanation of the rejection. He replied that my article was obviously facetious. I wrote back saying that of course it was, but wasn't this equally true of the article he had published? Why was he discriminating against me? I never received a reply. His morality didn't require that he provide one.

> MORAL: *Smoke gets in the eyes of scientists as*
> *well as in the eyes of people.*

Righteous indignation can perform miracles; for example, even
smoke that doesn't exist can get in the eyes of the indignant.

❦ ❦ ❦   *Allergic to Smoke*

*I was having dinner one night with friends in the smoking section of
an elegant restaurant. Pipe smoking was still permitted then. At the
end of the meal, when coffee was served, I pulled out my pipe to make
it ready for use. A short while later a waitress came up to me and,
with embarrassment, asked if I would mind not smoking. I asked why;
wasn't I in the smoking section? Yes, she said, but the woman sitting
at the table behind me was allergic to smoke and was reacting badly
to it. She had asked the waitress to ask me to stop smoking. I asked
why the lady had not been seated in the nonsmoking section. The
waitress told me it had been full at the time. Alright, I said, I would
stop smoking on one condition: the waitress would have to give my
pipe to the lady it offended. When I tried to hand the waitress my pipe
she drew back. I told her I would not stop smoking unless she gave it
to the lady. With great reluctance she took the pipe from me, looked
at it with surprise, and exclaimed that it had not been lighted. Right,
I said, that's why I want you to give it to the lady. She didn't, but
she did tell her what had happened. The lady rose indignantly and
stormed out of the restaurant.*

> MORAL: **The trouble with morality is that it**
> **obscures the difference between good and evil.**

I had a similar experience on an elevator in an office building
in New York. Carrying an unlighted pipe in my mouth, I entered an elevator occupied by two elderly women. One of the
women told me that smoking was not allowed on elevators. I
told her I was aware of that but I was not smoking: my pipe
was neither filled nor lighted. Then why, she wanted to know,

was I carrying it in my mouth? I told her I carried it in my mouth because I wanted to. She then informed me that I had no right to do so and demanded that I remove it immediately.

The current righteousness directed by neoprohibitionists against alcohol is another case in point. Neoprohibitionists have no pangs of conscience when they distort data to prove their point or omit data that disprove it. For example, they insist on treating alcohol as though it were an illegal, addictive drug. They ignore the fact that its use is legal and that, unlike addictive drugs, it is beneficial to one's health when used in moderation. They also fail to observe that any substance—sugar, milk, aspirin, salt, meat, and so on—when used immoderately is harmful to one's health. They ignore the fact that most teenagers drink, and therefore that efforts to keep them from starting to drink are too late. They also ignore the fact that youngsters who are permitted to drink mildly alcoholic beverages with their families at meals or ceremonial occasions are less likely to grow into alcohol abusers than youngsters to whom alcohol is forbidden.

I am offended by the neoprohibitionists, but not because I drink heavily or regularly and am trying to rationalize my habit. I rarely drink alcoholic beverages, but my abstention is not for moral reasons. I simply don't like most of them. Furthermore, my wife and I recently suffered severe physical damage when we were struck by a drunk driver while crossing a street on foot. I have no sympathy for the abusers of alcohol. But I also have no sympathy for those who abuse the nonabusive users of alcohol.

It strikes me as curious that precisely when the so-called moral majority attained its greatest political clout, we had the greatest number of cases of immorality in the body politic. Furthermore, some of the worst infractions of common morality were made by those who have derived their incomes from preaching morality in the name of God. I am sympathetic with the old Negro spiritual that says, "Ev'rybody talking 'bout heab'n ain't goin' dere."

The principal benefit of travel, and more so of *living* abroad, is that it enables us to get glimpses of ourselves as others see us, and to realize that others' views are more accurate than ours. Progress begins with grasping the truth about ourselves, however unpleasant it may be. Unfortunately, few things are more difficult than this. Perhaps the only thing that is more difficult is to change ourselves in ways indicated by that truth once it is perceived.

Notes

Chapter 2

1. Silberman, 1970, p. 10.
2. Herndon, 1971, p. 19.
3. Illich, 1972, p. 1.
4. *Newsweek*, February 16, 1970, p. 69.
5. *The National Commission on Excellence in Education*, 1983, p. 1.
6. Brimelow, 1983, p. 61.
7. Livingston, 1971, p. 91.
8. Schon, 1971, p. 50.
9. Brimelow, 1983, p. 62.
10. Brimelow, 1983, p. 64.
11. Jenks, 1970.
12. Mehta, 1979, p. 5.
13. Nicholson and Lorenzo, 1981, pp. 66–67.

Chapter 3

1. Ireson, 1959, p. 507
2. Wolfle, 1971.
3. See Ackoff, 1971, and Ackoff and Vergara, 1981.
4. Henry, 1963, p. 288.
5. Laing, 1967, pp. 71–72.
6. Quittenton, 1972, p. 9.

Chapter 4

1. Laing, 1967, pp. 93–94.
2. Laing, 1967, pp. 90–91.
3. Finnie, 1970.

Chapter 5

1. *The American Heritage Dictionary*, Dell, 1976.
2. Churchman, 1985, p. 257.
3. Beer, 1966.

Bibliography

Ackoff, R.L. *The Art of Problem Solving*. John Wiley & Sons, New York, 1978.

———, and Elsa Vergara. "Creativity in Problem Solving and Planning: a Review." *European Journal of Operational Research*, 7 (1981):1–13.

Beer, Stafford. *Decision and Control*. John Wiley & Sons, London, 1966.

Brimelow, P. "What to Do about America's Schools." *Fortune*, September 1983:60–67.

Churchman, C.W. "Churchman's Conversations." *Systems Research*, 2 (1985):257–258.

Finnie, W. *Toward a Systems Analysis of Racial Equality*. Ph.D. dissertation in operations research, University of Pennsylvania, Philadelphia, 1970.

Henry, J. *Culture against Man*. Random House, New York, 1963.

Herndon, J. *How to Survive in Your Native Land*. Simon & Schuster, New York, 1971.

Illich, I. *Deschooling Society*. Harrow Books, New York, 1972.

Ireson, W.G. "Preparation for Business in Engineering Schools." *The*

Education of American Businessmen, F.C. Pierson et al, McGraw-Hill Book Co., New York, 1959:507.

Jenks, C. "Giving Parents Money for Schooling: Educational Vouchers." *Phi Delta Kappa*, September 1970:49–52.

Laing, R. *The Politics of Experience*. Ballantine Books, New York, 1967.

Livingston, S.J. "Myth of the Well-Educated Manager." *Harvard Business Review*, January-February 1971:91–101.

Mehta, P. "Participation of Rural Poor in Rural Development." *IFDA Dossier*, no. 9 (July 1979):1–8.

Newsweek, "What's Wrong With the High Schools?" February 16, 1970, 69.

Nicholson, S., and S. Lorenzo. "The Political Implication of Child Participation: Steps toward a Participatory Society." *IFDA Dossier*, no. 22 (March-April 1981):65–70.

Quittenton, R.C. "Forum." *University Affairs*, October 1972:9.

Schon, D. *Beyond the Stable State*. Random House, New York, 1971.

Silberman, C. *Crisis in Classrooms*. Random House, New York, 1970.

The National Commission on Excellence in Education. "A Nation at Risk: The Imperative for Educational Reform." *The Chronicle of Higher Education*, May 4, 1983:11–16.

Wolfle, Dael. "Editorial." *Science*, 173 (July 9, 1971):109.